Word Nerds

Teaching All Students to Learn and Love Vocabulary

Stenhouse

PUBLISHERS

www.stenhouse.com

Portland, Maine

Brenda J. **Overturf** • Leslie H. **Montgomery** • Margot Holmes **Smith**

Stenhouse Publishers
www.stenhouse.com

Library of Congress Cataloging-in-Publication Data
Overturf, Brenda J.
  Word nerds : teaching all students to learn and love vocabulary / Brenda J. Overturf, Leslie H. Montgomery, and Margot Holmes Smith.
    pages cm
  Includes bibliographical references and index.
  ISBN 978-1-57110-954-5 (pbk. : alk. paper) -- ISBN 978-1-57110-979-8 (e-book) 1. Vocabulary--Study and teaching. I. Montgomery, Leslie H., 1949- II. Holmes Smith, Margot. III. Title.
  LB1574.5.O84 2013
  372.44--dc23
                                                                    2012037542

Cover photograph by Angela Shoemaker
Cover design, interior design, and typesetting by designboy Creative Group

Manufactured in the United States of America

PRINTED ON 30% PCW
RECYCLED PAPER

19 18   9 8 7 6

For our students,
who continue to inspire us
every day

Contents

Acknowledgments

No book happens without the support and encouragement of others. We were lucky enough to have a wonderful principal, Dr. Dewey Hensley, who believed in us and expected us to change the lives of our students. We will be forever grateful to him and his confidence in our kids. Our literacy coach, Lori Atherton, has been an amazing source of ideas, information, and support. Thank you to Ashlee Kemper, our colleague and cheerleader, for demonstrating that strategic vocabulary instruction can work with early primary English learners. We would like to thank Holly Holland, our editor-extraordinaire at Stenhouse, as well as Philippa Stratton, Stenhouse's editorial director, whose enthusiasm for this project, encouragement to blend our voices, and close attention to detail made this a better book. We are grateful to our colleagues in the literacy field who have researched and written about vocabulary instruction, and provided a solid base for this work. Finally, we truly appreciate our colleagues at Atkinson, the University of Louisville, Jefferson County Public Schools, and surrounding school districts who have supported us and believed in thoughtful and intentional vocabulary instruction for student success.

Brenda: I would like to thank my daughter, Whitney, for inspiring me with her insatiable love for life and teaching me what it means to be an author, and my son, Drew, for his adventurous spirit and reminding me to always, always dream big. I am grateful to my parents, Paul and Nancy Scott, and my sisters, Dana Latorre and Karen Small, for being proud of my accomplishments and supporting my professional life. My coauthors, Leslie and Margot, are not only two of the most talented teachers I know but also delightful to work with. Thanks go to Jill Wells, for her help with the beginning research on this book, and to Trish Priddy, for her close review of and enthusiasm for the manuscript. But mostly I would like to thank Jim, who understood my writing schedule even when it kept me locked in my office, and who always made sure I had that little dish of ice cream when I really needed it.

Leslie: Thank you to my teacher parents (my dad, Martin Montgomery, my mom, Linda Brumback, and my second mother, Peggy Yusk) for instilling in me my passion for teaching and my work ethic. I am who I am because of the love, humor, and support of my sisters, Lisa Potter and Leah McMahan, and their families. I am grateful to Margot Holmes Smith, my dear friend and colleague, for never giving up, validating ALL of my emotions, and keeping us laughing! Thank you to Brenda Overturf for insisting that this book become a reality and always believing in us. To all of my friends who have put up with me while I have been on this teaching journey, you truly are the best! I will be forever grateful for my first group of students at Atkinson, who touched me so deeply with their courage, wit, and beautiful hearts. They always motivated me to grow as an educator to meet their needs. Thank you to Stacie, Demetria, Madison, Olivia, Dante, Katlin, Alexis, Daniel, Tristen, Todd, Davion, Tayaunna, Charron, Alfontanae, DeJaynae, and all of my students throughout the years!

Margot: First, I would like to thank my two beautiful twin daughters, Jordynn and Jalynn, for inspiring me to step outside of my comfort zone and soar to new heights in my career. Next, I would like to thank my parents and brother for always supporting and encouraging me to be the best that I can be. I would like to thank my husband, Ronnie, for being the one to encourage me to go back to school and earn my degree in teaching. I would also like to thank my friend and colleague Leslie Montgomery for embarking on this teaching journey with me. Thank you for always being patient and flexible during the most challenging times of our careers. Thank you for not letting me give up at times when I felt I could not do this anymore. I would like to thank Brenda for seeing my potential as an educator and for providing opportunities that have allowed me to grow professionally and personally. Finally, I would like to thank my students for allowing me to try new things and learn and grow from my mistakes. Never let anyone stop you from achieving your dreams and reaching your highest potential. Remember to never say "can't," because you CAN!

Introduction

I scurried down the hallway at Atkinson Academy for Excellence in Teaching and Learning toward Margot Holmes's third-grade classroom on an early November day. Colorful samples of student work decorated the halls, and out in the paved courtyard vibrant leaves whirled and danced. Margot had prepared me for my visit to her classroom in an impoverished urban neighborhood, telling me that she and her students would be working on vocabulary instruction. I slipped into the room, expecting to see a good but isolated vocabulary activity, the type of lesson I usually saw when teachers told me they were "doing vocabulary." This time was much different, however.

Margot greeted me with a nod and went on with her lesson. Students began to smile in anticipation as Margot projected a screen saver of multicolored wavy lines on the electronic whiteboard at the front of the room. When she clicked on the sound function on her laptop, a rap beat permeated the classroom and the wavy lines pulsated in time to the music. Students started tapping their feet, clapping their hands, and swaying their bodies to the music. Margot called out, "Don't forget, first we are doing the synonyms and then the antonyms."

She started a rap in time to the music. Margot called out the first part of each verse, and the students finished the phrase by shouting the synonym or example of the word. It went like this:

When I say "DIVERSITY,"
You say "DIFFERENT."

When I say "LANGUAGES,"
You say "SPEAK."

When I say "NEIGHBORING,"
You say "NEAR."

When I say "SETTLEMENT,"
You say "VILLAGE."

When I say "TERRITORY,"
You say "LAND."

After these verses, they changed to antonyms/non-examples.

Students chanted in rhythm, moving their bodies to the beat, clearly enjoying themselves. It was obvious that they knew these words and this was part of a well-known routine. My mind started racing. Where did Margot get this activity? What else did she do as part of vocabulary instruction?

When I talked with Margot after the lesson, I learned that she and her teammate, Leslie Montgomery, were working together to implement a weekly plan to teach vocabulary in their primary classrooms. These two teachers had found a way to work vocabulary instruction into their daily schedules and were following a systematic method of helping their students experience academic vocabulary and concept words in order to increase their achievement. They were using multisensory instruction that included music, art, movement, drama, writing, comprehension skills, test-taking skills, and technology. And their standardized test results demonstrated that their kids were learning well. They seemed to have an inspiring story worth telling.

The School

Leslie and Margot teach at one of the highest-poverty public elementary schools in Kentucky. About 90 percent of Atkinson's students are eligible for free lunch, and another 4 percent are eligible for reduced lunch. Forty-three percent of the students are African American, and 46 percent are white. Many children who attend Atkinson face challenges outside school that are often associated with community poverty: hunger; homelessness; parent incarceration; adults with no jobs or low-paying jobs; poor health, including alcoholism, drug abuse, or mental health issues; and domestic and community violence. Atkinson is designated as the "highest needs" school in Jefferson County, which includes Louisville. The school district serves 97,000 students in 154 schools.

From 2003 to 2009 Atkinson was a Reading First school. Under the federal No Child Left Behind Act of 2001, Reading First grants required schools to purchase research-based reading programs that followed the guidelines of the National Reading Panel (NRP) report (National Institute of Child Health and Human Development 2000). The NRP report discussed the importance of instruction in phonemic awareness, phonics, fluency, vocabulary, and comprehension. Although critics of the NRP report pointed out the lack of focus on other factors, such as writing, family literacy, and independent reading, Reading First teachers were required to implement their school's chosen reading program with little deviation.

The Atkinson Reading First grant was initially awarded for a schoolwide scripted program based on grouping and regrouping for ninety minutes each day. When a dynamic new principal came on board and found that there had been no progress in literacy development during the three years the program had been implemented, he sought permission from the Kentucky Department of Education to switch to a program that included writing instruction and a deeper emphasis on reading comprehension. Like most purchased reading programs, however, the new one still included very little emphasis on vocabulary instruction.

Leslie and Margot were hired as first-year teachers at Atkinson just as the ineffective reading program was replaced. The principal encouraged them to use their own professional judgment to plan best practice instruction for high-risk students. At the same time, they participated in mandated professional development focusing on Reading First strategies and administered the required standardized assessments.

The Teachers

I first met Margot and Leslie in 2006 when they were students in my elementary preservice language arts class as part of the Master of Arts in Teaching (MAT) program at the University of Louisville. The MAT program is an accelerated program for graduate students who already have a bachelor's degree and want to become teachers. Vocabulary development was included in the course work, but because of limited time it was only one small piece of the literacy focus.

Leslie was born into a family of teachers, but tried other careers first before enrolling in the MAT program. Margot started out to become a dentist, but later decided to follow her mother's path into teaching as well. After completing the MAT program together, Leslie and Margot were both hired at Atkinson.

They entered their first classrooms full of optimism and enthusiasm, but reality soon tempered their high spirits. Both teachers realized their students had a severely limited knowledge of academic vocabulary and consequently had a difficult time remembering the words used in science, mathematics, and social studies lessons. The students also grappled with concept words and descriptive words in everyday conversations. Sensing that these gaps were hindering students' success in school, Leslie and Margot wanted to improve their vocabulary instruction and assessment but did not know how.

As Margot said, "My first year of teaching I simply gave the students words and the definitions and they recorded it in a notebook. They would draw a picture and write a sentence, but that was about it. I would give a test each Friday where they had to write the word and definition. Students may have retained *a few* of the words that year, but because they weren't taking ownership and having to use the words on a daily basis I didn't feel that my vocabulary instruction was effective."

Low student achievement results supported that hunch, so Leslie and Margot launched a quest for better methods.

Crafting a Vocabulary Plan

After their first year of teaching, Leslie and Margot participated in the Kentucky Reading Project, a state literacy professional development initiative for elementary teachers. I directed the program at the University of Louisville. The Kentucky Reading Project was a two-week immersion into current literacy practices, with follow-up professional development and classroom visits during the school year. We spent a day on research-based vocabulary instruction for elementary students and shared vocabulary strategies. Later that same summer, Leslie and Margot also attended a district professional development session on vocabulary instruction where district presenters shared an idea for a three-day plan for vocabulary instruction targeting the needs of primary students. In this plan, teachers would introduce words on the first day, engage students in enjoyable vocabulary activities that included synonyms and antonyms on the second day, and review and assess the words on the third day. As part of the presentation, the facilitators showed a video clip of Lori Mardis, a local teacher whose featured vocabulary lesson included an activity she called "Vocabulary Party."

As Leslie and Margot talked about the professional development ideas, they realized that the children in their classrooms needed vocabulary instruction every day. The two teachers spent most of the summer figuring out how to fit daily vocabulary work into a literacy schedule already packed with read-alouds, shared reading, guided reading groups, self-selected reading, instruction in word recognition, and writing. They discussed what words to choose, how to get their kids motivated to learn, what activities they could use, and how to physically rearrange their classrooms so that all these activities could take place. They approached the new school year with a plan and renewed enthusiasm for teaching.

When I entered Margot's classroom the following November for a coaching visit and saw students engaged in a vocabulary rap, the vocabulary plan was in full swing. Leslie had started teaching second grade at Atkinson but later looped with her students and was now teaching on a third-grade team with Margot. I was intrigued by their methods of teaching vocabulary to a fragile population and was impressed by the command of academic vocabulary their students already displayed. As the former district coordinator of reading instruction and assessment and now a literacy instructor at the university, I was familiar with the research on vocabulary development and the importance of vocabulary instruction and assessment, especially for students from high-poverty families and those with limited English proficiency. I knew that vocabulary instruction had received a new focus at the elementary level after the publication of the National Reading Panel Report in 2000 and as part of the federal Reading First grant program. Because of my school district position, I had visited hundreds of elementary classrooms, yet I had never seen such engaging, systematic vocabulary instruction as in Margot and Leslie's classes.

I asked to spend some sustained time in their classrooms, and Leslie, Margot, and their principal, Dr. Dewey Hensley, welcomed me. I visited their classrooms many times that school year and along with their school reading coach, Lori Atherton, and a district literacy coach, Maria Carrico, reviewed their required reading assessment data. After Leslie and Margot had implemented their vocabulary plan for one year, their students were scoring higher in vocabulary than all other third-grade Reading First classrooms in the school district.

I spent another eighteen months with these teachers and students at Atkinson. Together we continued to refine their vocabulary plan. Students demonstrated continued success in classroom and standardized tests. I observed vocabulary instruction and how the students reacted.

I was there the day Leslie said to the class, "Let's play a little *Deal or No Deal* to practice our words," and Dante looked up, made eye contact with Leslie, and exclaimed with confidence, "I'm already on it!"

I remember with a chuckle the day Margot's kids played a carefully planned trick on me. They looked like pitiful puppies as Margot sadly explained that they had all failed their vocabulary assessment the week before. Then they laughed hysterically and called out "You got schooled!" when I fell for the ruse (actually each of them had scored well).

I was also there the day the science lab teacher, Heather Gregg Lynd, came into Leslie's classroom specifically to tell me in front of the students that they were "blowing the top off" the vocabulary in the science classroom because of the word connections they were making.

Margot and Leslie kept journals of their vocabulary teaching. We examined student work samples together. We had a professional discussion each time I visited and talked about ways to enhance what they were already doing well. Leslie again looped with her students, now to fourth grade. Her students were familiar with systematic vocabulary instruction by then, and we considered how she could nurture her intermediate students to an even higher level of vocabulary development.

I recruited Leslie and Margot to present a session on their vocabulary plan for a local Louisville Writing Project conference, for my graduate school classes, and for my next year's Kentucky Reading Project cohort. At each venue, experienced and novice teachers were enthralled and asked Margot and Leslie to share their plan with their faculties. In my visits to other classrooms, I saw Margot and Leslie's vocabulary plan being implemented in a bordering school district that is one of the highest-scoring in the state, in a neighboring rural school, and in other schools throughout our urban school district. Teachers serving varied populations of students reported that their kids were also engaged and retaining essential vocabulary as a result of this instruction. Margot and Leslie next won a district Teaching Innovation Award for their vocabulary plan. They accepted their award at a ceremony held at the Muhammad Ali Center in Louisville, with Muhammad Ali and his wife looking on.

Speaking of Success

In order to receive federal Reading First grants in 2002, states had to commit to assess phonemic awareness, phonics, fluency, vocabulary, and comprehension. In our state, a standardized reading test called the Group Reading Assessment and Diagnostic Evaluation (GRADE) was administered three times a year in schools such as Atkinson that received the Reading First grants. Although the test was a measure of knowledge, it was also a high-stakes assessment because program decisions were made based on the results.

According to district statistics, students in Leslie Montgomery and Margot Holmes's classes scored higher on the GRADE vocabulary subtest than students in other Reading First classrooms at their grade level. Additionally, their vocabulary results correlated with increases in reading comprehension achievement. When both teachers moved to the intermediate grades and no longer gave the GRADE test, they continued to teach strategic vocabulary instruction and their students' reading scores on state assessments soared. In 2011, most of the students in these two classes scored "proficient" or "distinguished," the two highest categories on the Kentucky Core Content Test for Reading.

What we describe in this book are methods based on extensive reading, discussion, and learning from others—researchers, colleagues, professional development providers, and students. Margot and Leslie certainly did not create all of their instructional strategies, and we have tried to credit sources wherever possible. For example, the vocabulary rap idea came from Andrea Marcum, an excellent music teacher at Arlington Elementary School in Lexington, who shared it at a Kentucky Reading Association conference session. Other ideas came to us from our literacy coach, who got them from state professional development sessions she attended when Atkinson was a Reading First school, or strategy-sharing sessions during our school district's summer institutes. Some of the strategies are backed by solid research and have been recommended for years by experts in the field. Leslie and Margot developed other strategies together, and the three of us collaborated to craft additional ones. Over time we designed the framework for a strategic vocabulary development plan that would support students from primary through intermediate grades. Although we began with grades two through five, we know teachers who have adapted the plan for kindergarten, grade one, and grade six.

Our purpose in writing this book is to highlight the importance of vocabulary development for all students, but especially for children of poverty. We know how capable and enthusiastic they are about word learning when their teachers provide the right scaffolding, tools, and support. Our dream is that all students will one day express the word confidence and ownership that third grader Matthew revealed when he exclaimed, "Yes! I am the *master* of synonyms and antonyms!" In short, we want our kids to be word nerds now so that they can grow up to be college graduates later.

Chapter 1

What's the Big Deal About Vocabulary Instruction?

All my life I've looked at words as though seeing them for the first time.
—Ernest Hemingway

In the first-year Spanish courses Brenda was required to take in college, she got to the point where she could pick up any Spanish text and read aloud with a fairly good accent and level of fluency. She sounded like she knew what she was doing. But here's her secret—she didn't understand all the words. In fact, she didn't understand many of them. She could usually get the gist of the passage, enough to know what the text was generally about but not enough to learn from it or explain it in detail. Sometimes she couldn't even get the gist. She was clueless until she learned strategies for making Spanish vocabulary her own.

This is how we imagine students must feel when they come to school with limited vocabulary knowledge. Like Bill Murray in the movie of the same name, our kids are "lost in translation." Look again at the quote at the beginning of the chapter. Although Hemingway was probably talking about looking at words anew in order to use them in a fresh and original way, the statement is literally true for students who encounter common school words for the first time. When teachers use words like *culture*, *magnet*, *divisor*, *expository*, *genetic*, and other subject-specific words and terms, many students have no context for understanding them. Texts of all kinds (print, visual, and digital) are filled with what could be fascinating ideas and information, but even if our kids are able to decode and pronounce the words, they may not understand their meaning without explicit vocabulary instruction. In addition, vocabulary deficits keep many students from demonstrating what they know on high-stakes standardized assessments because the questions use so many words they do not know.

We all need strategies to learn new vocabulary, no matter our ages or backgrounds. Think about a time you tried to learn something new. Maybe it was the art of French cooking or ocean kayaking. Maybe it was research about a new teaching method or a course in applied statistics for graduate school. In any case, we're sure there was specialized vocabulary involved. Unless we learn the terminology essential for understanding and expressing knowledge of a subject, we can't talk or write or perform with confidence. We must have the right words to draw on.

"School Talk" and High-Risk Students

Research has shown that a child's vocabulary knowledge is frequently tied to economic background. Hart and Risley (1995) conducted a major study of the number of words children learn by age three and found huge differences between those from affluent families and those from low-income families. The results were so startling that the report is often called the Meaningful Differences study because Hart and Risley wrote about a "30-million word gap" between children from professional families and children from economically disadvantaged households. The researchers found that the preschool word gap correlated with later school achievement; third-grade students who had higher-level vocabularies as preschoolers performed much better in school than students who had less-developed vocabulary knowledge in preschool. Other studies bolster the links among economic status, vocabulary knowledge, and later school achievement (Dickinson and Tabors 2002; White, Graves, and Slater 1990).

In his research about vocabulary, Keith Stanovich (1986) found that kids who have a solid word base get ahead faster and achieve more in school, while students with a less-developed vocabulary tend to progress more slowly. He called his theory the Matthew Effects (named after a verse in the book of Matthew), and hypothesized that "the rich get richer and the poor get poorer" because the vocabulary gap often actually widens as students advance through school.

With vocabulary instruction, we must sometimes teach a new word for a term the student already knows. Other times, we may be teaching new information and the new words that label the information. A concept is an idea or notion—a way to categorize information. Some concepts are familiar, but the word for the concept is unknown. For example, a child may understand the concept of rain (water falling from the sky) before he learns the words *rain*, *shower*, or *precipitation*. Some concepts are unfamiliar, and the student is faced with learning both the concept and the words that describe it at the same time; an example of this might be *water cycle*. High-poverty students can be compared with English language learners (ELLs) when it comes to vocabulary development. Both usually have to learn new concepts while dealing with unfamiliar language (Echevarria 1998).

Because there is such a strong correlation between vocabulary knowledge and reading comprehension (Anderson and Nagy 1991; Stahl and Fairbanks 1986), a focus on word knowledge is particularly important in a literacy program designed to help students living in poverty. Some teachers mistakenly believe that using simpler vocabulary in the classroom is the best way to serve students at risk of failure. For example, we have all known teachers who use the words *guess* instead of *hypothesize* or the phrase *words that sound like a sound* instead of *onomatopoeia*. Their intentions may be kindhearted (to make sure all the kids can understand the lesson), but the results can be disastrous. If students come to school with a limited vocabulary, where else but in our classrooms will they learn the words they need to be successful in life?

Research has shown that when it comes to risk factors for vocabulary development, poverty trumps race, urban versus rural community, limited English proficiency, and language impairments. Vocabulary interventions have to be powerful enough to accelerate, not just incrementally advance, word learning for students coming from low-income households to narrow the achievement gap (Marulis and Neuman 2011). As teachers and teacher-educators who work with high-risk populations, we believe it is our obligation to make sure students learn vocabulary that will empower them and help them overcome the circumstances of their birth. More than being kindhearted, this approach can truly be life-changing. We have seen children make up years of academic deficits by learning to read, speak, and write with strong word knowledge.

Connections to the Common Core State Standards

The Common Core State Standards Initiative (NGA/CCSSO 2010), led by the Council of Chief State School Officers and the National Governor's Association, aims to provide equal educational opportunities for all U.S. students and ensure they are prepared for college and careers. The goal was to develop a set of uniform academic standards for both English and mathematics based on research and international benchmarks. The standards, published in 2010, have been adopted by most states, the District of Columbia, and the U.S. Virgin Islands. Kentucky was the first state to assess the standards in 2012, but most states will not do so until the 2014–2015 school year.

The English Language Arts Standards include the same strands at each grade level, K–5:

- Reading: Literature
- Reading: Informational Text
- Reading: Foundational Skills
- Writing
- Speaking and Listening
- Language

Although we began our strategic vocabulary instruction plan well before the Common Core State Standards were published, we knew we were on the right track when we saw how prominently the standards focus on word knowledge. We were excited to see vocabulary connected to the standards in Reading, Writing, and an entire cluster on Vocabulary Acquisition and Use (Language). Because so much of our vocabulary instruction includes academic conversation, we believe the Speaking and Listening standards are also connected to vocabulary study.

From kindergarten (RL.K.4: "Ask and answer questions about unknown words in a text.") to grade five (RI.5.4: "Determine the meaning of general academic and domain-specific words and phrases in a text relevant to a grade five topic or subject area."), it is obvious that vocabulary is a vital part of the elementary reading standards. This makes sense, of course, because little or no comprehension occurs if the words are unfamiliar.

The standards for Writing also include references to appropriate vocabulary in producing writing pieces, especially informative/explanatory texts. For example, beginning at grade four, all students will be expected to, "Use precise language and domain-specific vocabulary to inform about or explain the topic" (W.4.2d and W.5.2d). Good writers make strategic word choices for their readers.

The bulk of expectations for vocabulary knowledge can be found in the "Vocabulary Acquisition and Use" cluster of the language standards. Each grade has at least three standards for vocabulary knowledge, with multiple indicators aligned with most of the goals. Across all grade levels students are expected to learn significant vocabulary in all content areas and be able to employ independent word-learning strategies.

Clearly, there are important reasons to provide comprehensive vocabulary instruction for high-risk learners. But how should we do this? In the rest of this book, we will describe our strategic vocabulary plan, and as we do so, we will show how we connect vocabulary instruction to the Common Core State Standards.

What Do We Know About Vocabulary Teaching and Learning?

Brenda's own first experiences teaching vocabulary could be a reality show called "What Not to Do." Brenda was an elementary teacher (first, second, and fifth grades) for ten years and then a middle school language arts teacher for another eight years before she left to focus on teacher learning. She is embarrassed to admit that for many of those years the most she did with explicit vocabulary instruction was to use the prevailing method of the day. That is, she gave her students a list of random words each week to look up in the dictionary and asked them to write the definition—exactly the way she had been taught in school. If she got really creative and asked students to use a vocabulary word in a sentence, she often got back something equally creative, such as *Mary forecasted her homework.* (Brenda could remotely see the student's logic—one definition of *forecast* is "to plan or arrange beforehand," but the sentence doesn't reflect an understanding of the word's preferred usage.) Each week Brenda dutifully constructed a vocabulary test, which required students to match a vocabulary word with its definition. Her students looked up definitions and wrote them in notebooks. Brenda created word lists, developed tests, and graded them. And guess what? Her students almost never transferred the new vocabulary words to their speaking or writing, which is the ultimate point of vocabulary instruction.

Brenda realized she was wasting her time and limiting her students' language acquisition because, clearly, something was wrong. She dropped the vocabulary lists and dictionary definitions. She began experimenting with unusual and high-utility words in the classroom. Like Janet Allen in *Words, Words, Words* (1999), she also expected her students to read and to read a lot. Brenda found out much later that these two activities are actually good vocabulary development strategies! As Allen said, "If I had to err, I'm glad I erred on the side of increasing reading time and abandoning what wasn't working" (10).

Brenda knew that vocabulary development was important; she just didn't know how to guide it well. She later found that she was not alone; many teachers need more information about effective vocabulary instruction (Bromley 2007).

Research Reveals the Right Approach

Over time, as we investigated ways to strengthen vocabulary instruction for our students and to verify the practices we were using, we discovered some essential ingredients for word study. Here are the key components:

1. Some words are more important to teach than others.
By some calculations, students will be asked to read more than 180,000 words throughout their K–12 education and will need to learn a reading vocabulary of 3,000–4,000 words each year (Graves 2006). How do teachers know what words to choose to teach? The thought is overwhelming!

In their wonderful book *Bringing Words to Life* (2002), Isabel Beck, Margaret McKeown, and Linda Kucan talk about levels of words that they call Tier One, Tier Two, and Tier Three. Tier One words are those that students already know when they come to school, words such as *clock*, *baby*, and *happy*. Tier Two words are high-frequency words students will likely encounter in their school reading yet probably don't know well. Tier Two words might include terms such as *coincidence*, *absurd*, *industrious*, and *fortunate*. Tier Three words are domain-specific words, such as *isotope*, *lathe*, *peninsula*, and *refinery*, which are primarily used in content areas. As the authors advise, Tier One words don't need to be taught explicitly because students already know them and Tier Three words should be introduced during content-area classes. Instead, they urge teachers to base most vocabulary instruction on Tier Two words.

2. Students have to learn words at more than one level.

Not all word knowledge is equal. Beck, McKeown, and Kucan (2002, 10) also talk about different levels of knowing words. A continuum of word knowledge would look like this (emphasis and interpretation added):

- No knowledge. (*I've never heard or seen the word.*)
- General sense of the word. (*I've seen or heard the word before.*)
- Narrow, context-bound knowledge. (*Although a word may have several meanings, I only know one meaning in one situation.*)
- Having knowledge of a word, but not being able to apply it readily enough to use in appropriate situations. (*I may know the word has several meanings, but because I'm not sure which one to use, I sometimes use the word the wrong way.*)
- Rich, decontextualized knowledge of a word's meaning, its relationship to other words, and its extension to metaphorical uses. (*I know multiple meanings of the word, and I can use the word appropriately in different situations.*)

Students need to learn words deeply to get to the most sophisticated level of vocabulary knowledge. When students are first introduced to a word, they can quickly get a sense of the word's meaning. Carey (1978) called this "fast-mapping" and explained that while fast-mapping begins the process of learning a word, it is not enough to help students develop full meaning and use. "Extended-mapping," where students get to the richer, deeper level of word use, takes more meaningful instruction.

3. Students learn words when they experience them multiple times.

To really learn a word, students need multiple exposures to it over time (Stahl 2003). How many times does a word need to be experienced before it is learned? Jenkins, Stein, and Wysocki (1984) found that students need at least six exposures to learn a word, while McKeown, Beck, Ormanson, and Pople (1985) found that it took twelve exposures. A systematic vocabulary plan can provide a sufficient number of exposures to new words over time.

4. Asking students to look up words in the dictionary and write the definition does not help them learn words.

Dictionary definitions may actually cloud a word's meaning rather than help a student learn it. Beck, McKeown, and Kucan (2002) discussed studies asking students to create sentences using dictionary definitions of words. Miller and Gildea (1985) found that 63 percent of the students' responses were judged to be "odd." Scott and Nagy (1989) found that students frequently interpreted one or two words from a dictionary definition as the entire meaning, and McKeown (1993) found that 60 percent of students' responses using dictionary definitions were unacceptable.

One important caveat is worth noting: Introducing words using student-friendly definitions in plain, everyday language does help students learn new vocabulary (Beck, McKeown, and Kucan 2002).

5. When students learn words, they build patterns and networks of meaning called "word schemas."

Nagy and Scott (1990) discussed various kinds of knowledge that can be applied in learning new vocabulary. Students make connections to their own background knowledge when deciding what a new word means. They connect the word to terms they already know. Sometimes they understand a synonym or antonym. Sometimes they use knowledge of prefixes, suffixes, and root words. These patterns of word learning are called "word schemas" (the plural of the word schema is actually *schemata*, but many people, including Nagy and Scott, just say, "schemas").

When Molly encounters an unknown word in a text, for example, she doesn't have to guess every word in the English language to figure it out. Instead, she activates her word schema about the type of word that would make sense in the context. Subconsciously, her brain begins to race: *Based on what I know about the structure of the English language, would this word most likely be a noun, a verb, or another type of word? Does the word have a prefix or a suffix? What do the prefix and suffix mean? What does the root mean? Have I seen the word used somewhere before? How does the word connect with other words I know? What are words that would make sense in this sentence?* Molly's brain can quickly narrow down her choices for what the right word might be. She can then hypothesize (infer) about the meaning of a particular word.

This is what it means to infer the meaning of a word from context. Students with well-developed word schemas can figure out the meaning of many words through use of sentence context. However, students with sparse word schemas cannot infer context as well.

In our thinking about strategic vocabulary, we connect the word *schema* to the idea of making connections in comprehension instruction. A *schema* is a framework for understanding. When we help build and activate students' word schemas, their vocabulary knowledge grows exponentially.

6. Students can learn some words through the use of wide reading.

For students who have learned to read, wide reading of different types of texts, including trade books, along with direct teacher instruction and rich vocabulary experiences can help them continue to build word schema (Anderson 1990; Nagy and Herman 1987).

For younger children, most vocabulary learning through reading has to be facilitated by adults and older peers because books for early readers intentionally contain simple words that children already know. Engaging students in various types of vocabulary activities by reading aloud texts with more sophisticated words that they will encounter in future texts will help them build their experiences with words and increase their word schemas (Beck and McKeown 2001; Biemiller and Boote 2006).

7. Students can learn some words through rich conversations with adults and peers. Students at risk for academic failure, including children of poverty, minority students, and English language learners, should participate in academic discussions on a regular basis. Researchers at the Center for Research in Education, Diversity, and Excellence (CREDE) at the University of California-Berkeley have found that culturally diverse learners need to be engaged in conversations with adults and peers in ways that can help them make connections, learn new concepts, and learn the words for those concepts.

Instructional conversation is a research-based strategy for encouraging academic discussion with diverse students (Goldenberg 1991; Tharp and Gallimore 1988). In an instructional conversation, teachers plan a theme and decide what they want students to know at the end of the discussion, but they also structure the discussion so that students can do most of the talking. During the instructional conversation, teachers weave in the background knowledge the students need and address skills or concepts directly when necessary. They ask open-ended questions, restate a student comment, pause strategically, or ask students to elaborate on an answer. They promote the students' bases for statements or opinions by asking questions such as, "What makes you think that?" (Goldenberg 1991).

By engaging in instructional conversation about vocabulary across content areas, students are able to explore new concepts as well. Instructional conversations can be a powerful instructional tool for helping students develop comprehension and extended word networks, whether planned for whole-group lessons or small-group work.

Another way to get students discussing vocabulary is through interactive read-alouds of children's literature and nonfiction texts that contain thought-provoking vocabulary. Hayes and Ahrens (1988) estimate that children's literature, with the exception of texts that have been simplified for beginning or inexperienced readers, contains two times as many rare words (those not found in the top ten thousand most frequently used words in the language) as in a conversation between two college-educated adults and more than all adult conversation except in courtroom testimony! The number of rare words found in adult television speech is not much more than adult conversation.

Consider this sentence from the children's picture book *A Bad Case of Stripes* (1998) by David Shannon:

The Creams were swamped with all kinds of remedies from psychologists, allergists, herbalists, nutritionists, psychics, an old medicine man, a guru, and even a veterinarian. Each so-called cure only added to poor Camilla's strange appearance until it was hard to even recognize her.

What a wealth of words! When teachers read aloud children's literature with attention-grabbing vocabulary and engage students in interactive discussions about some of the rare words heard in the text, they can help students extend their vocabulary schemas (Beck and McKeown 2001).

8. Students can learn some words through word play.

We want to help our students develop the habit of being curious about words. Innate curiosity and the motivation to take risks with new words can be the beginnings of word consciousness (Graves 2006).

Students need many opportunities to play with words. Lane and Allen (2010) discuss how to develop word consciousness in kindergarten, where young children learn to use sophisticated vocabulary ("The weather today is rather brisk!") in their classroom. Blachowicz and Fisher (2009) talk about promoting vocabulary through word play using word books, games, art, music, and drama.

Instruction where students are moving and interacting is often called "multisensory teaching." It involves a combination of visual, auditory, kinesthetic, and tactile (VAKT) activities to address the learning styles of all students. Multisensory teaching has been found to be effective with diverse learners in literacy instruction (International Dyslexia Association 2009; Reinhart and Martinez 1996; Wadlington 2000). Vocabulary instruction that includes multisensory activity can help students internalize new words and continue to develop word schema. Besides, it creates novelty and excitement about words—a sure-fire motivator.

9. Students can learn some words by direct instruction.

There are obviously too many words in the English language to teach all of them individually, but Stahl and Fairbanks (1986) found that direct vocabulary teaching of some words can enhance achievement. Robert Marzano (2009) has found positive results in experimental research on students learning individual vocabulary words when teachers use this six-step instructional plan:

1. Provide a description, explanation, or example of the new term.
2. Ask students to restate the description, explanation, or example in their own words.
3. Ask students to construct a picture, pictograph, or symbolic representation of the term.
4. Engage students periodically in activities that help them add to their knowledge of the term in their vocabulary notebooks.

5. Periodically ask students to discuss the term with one another.
6. Involve students periodically in games that enable them to play with the term.

Some students, especially those with culturally and linguistically diverse backgrounds, need to be taught individual words, either because they are learning English as an additional language or because they come from home and community environments where academic language is seldom used. Marzano's steps to vocabulary learning can be used as a model for teaching individual words.

10. Most students need word-learning strategies to become independent readers.
Students must be able to determine the meanings of unfamiliar words without help when reading independently. One way to decide what a word means is to use context clues. Teaching students to use sentence and passage level context clues enables them to approach unknown words in a strategic way.

Students also need appropriate instruction in morphology. Here's an example: a *morpheme* is "the smallest unit of meaning," and *ology* means "the study of." The word *morphology* means "the study of the smallest units of meaning." When students learn morphology, they find a key to unlock the meanings of longer, multisyllabic words. According to the Common Core State Standards, as early as kindergarten children should learn common inflectional suffixes to show plural or past tense (e.g., *-s, -es, -ed*). From there, students should learn the meanings of common derivational affixes that portray their own meaning, such as *un-* (not), *pre-* (before), and *-ful* (full). Beginning in fourth grade, students should learn the meanings of appropriate Greek and Latin roots such as *photo* (light), *therm* (heat), and *port* (to carry). Knowing the meanings of these small pieces of words will help students put together much of the puzzle of the English language. An excellent resource for the teaching of morphology is found in *Words Their Way* by Bear, Invernizzi, Templeton, and Johnston (2008).

A Need for Systematic Vocabulary Instruction

Every December for the last fifteen-plus years, Jack Cassidy has written a "What's Hot, What's Not" column for *Reading Today*, the International Reading Association's monthly newspaper. To prepare for the column, Cassidy asks experts in the field of literacy to list topics they feel are "hot," "should be hot," "not hot," "should not be hot." For 2011, unchanged from the last several years, vocabulary/word meaning was rated "hot" and the experts agreed it should be "very hot."

There is a good reason for this. Systematic vocabulary instruction has often been recommended as a way to address the achievement gap (Beck, McKeown, and Kucan 2002; Lovelace and Stewart 2009; Marzano 2004; Stone and Urquhart 2008; White and Kim

2009), yet it still doesn't happen often in classrooms. Although more than one hundred years of research supports the importance of vocabulary instruction for student success (Graves 2006), most teachers still provide very little direct vocabulary instruction (Beck, McKeown, and Kucan 2002; Watts 1995). Reading First grants mandated that vocabulary be taught in K–3 classrooms, but a follow-up study showed that teachers concentrated much more on phonemic awareness and fluency than on vocabulary instruction (White and Kim 2009). We believe this is because teachers often receive very little guidance on how to effectively teach vocabulary.

What should a systematic vocabulary plan include? Beck, McKeown, and Kucan (2002) describe a five-day plan using "robust vocabulary instruction." Michael Graves (2006) recommends a four-part vocabulary program to address the varied needs of students who have limited word knowledge, English language learners, children who possess an adequate but not outstanding vocabulary base, and students who already have high-level word knowledge and require challenge to develop further. In *The Vocabulary Book*, Graves (2006) includes these four parts to the plan: (1) provide rich and varied language experiences, (2) teach individual words, (3) teach word-learning strategies, and (4) promote word consciousness.

In this book, we borrow the structure of Graves's four-part vocabulary program (see Figure 1.1), but we concentrate on individual word instruction and word-learning strategies within a larger literacy framework. We also follow the guidelines of Frey and Fisher (2009) when they state that teachers should make teaching vocabulary *intentional, transparent, useable, personal,* and *a priority*. Although some of the strategies we use are original, and some were found in vocabulary resources, all the components of our vocabulary plan are based on supportive research.

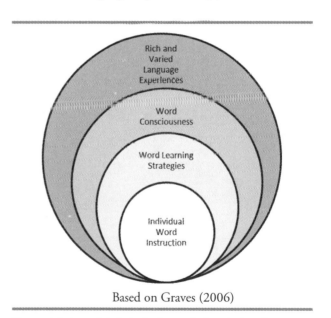

Based on Graves (2006)

Figure 1.1 *A model of strategic vocabulary instruction*

Passage to Progress

For students who arrive at school with a limited "school talk" background, systematic vocabulary instruction opens a door to a secret world. As teachers, we unlock the door and nudge it open. We show our students what is possible and encourage them to step through. Then we open the door a little wider. Students tiptoe into the unknown and look around. They try on the new world of words for size. Along the way, they may find high weeds and loose stones, forbidding fences and deep ditches. We continue to nurture and provide support until students can venture out on their own, knowing how to circumvent the obstacles and approach the challenges they encounter. Soon students who had little fluency with academic language can discuss and write about concepts in a whole new way. They become part of what Frank Smith calls the "literacy club" (Smith 1987). They sound as intelligent as they are and become an accepted part of an educated group because they can participate in an academic conversation and make connections to subject concepts. They have "word confidence."

The rest of this book is devoted to describing the vocabulary plan that Margot and Leslie use in their classrooms every day. We will show how the plan connects to research outlined in this chapter and explain how teachers can help all students skillfully and enthusiastically learn language.

Chapter 2

Classrooms That Foster Word Confidence

Demetria: Hey, Ms. Montgomery. Guess what?
Leslie: What?
Demetria: My mom and me went to Gatti-land last night.
Leslie: That sounds intriguing!
Demetria: I told my mom they had a variety of pizza and games there. Then I asked my mom if she knew what the word *variety* meant. She did!

If we want classrooms where students like Demetria delight in using and celebrating vivacious vocabulary, we must encourage playfulness with words. Children who come to our classrooms with limited word banks are often afraid to experiment with language, primarily because using unfamiliar words takes them out of their comfort zones. We need to make sure that they feel safe to take risks. Teachers set the tone by being respectful of children's questions and attempts to use new words. They establish routines that encourage discovery and self-reliance. They honor effort and celebrate mastery. They spark academic conversations that provide good models of vocabulary use and much-needed practice, enabling students to talk confidently with the teacher and with their peers.

The Importance of Routine

Students from impoverished families often must cope with so much chaos in their lives that school becomes one of the few structured places where they can feel secure. Establishing daily and weekly routines helps them gain a sense of belonging to a community. The consistency announces, "This is the way we do things here so everyone can learn."

When we say "routine," we want to make it clear that we are not advocating boring, mind-numbing instructional activities in the classroom. Far from it! But our students do need us to plan certain practices they can count on. Clear and consistent expectations give them confidence and order. As Leslie puts it, "Routine acts as an anchor for our kids. It is something to ground them and for them to hold on to as they try things they didn't know existed."

We begin each year by practicing the procedures they will need in our classrooms. A few days before beginning vocabulary study, for example, we read aloud various children's books, such as *Miss Alaineus: A Vocabulary Disaster* (Frasier 2000) and *Thesaurus Rex* (Steinberg 2005). The classroom conversation generated by these read-alouds helps us begin a dialogue with students about the importance of vocabulary development. Next, we spend several weeks modeling how we want our students to engage in vocabulary instruction.

"At first, I spend a large portion of my reading block just introducing students to the routines and procedures of vocabulary," explains Margot. "I also believe it is important for me to show I am passionate and serious about teaching vocabulary in order for my students to take it seriously."

Taking time to establish routines, such as how students will complete vocabulary journals and practice new words, is beneficial in the long run. Class activities can progress more quickly when students know what to expect. At the same time, we must ensure that our routines are not so rigid that they ignore the needs of our students. Leslie clarifies, "I believe in listening to the kids and being tuned to the vibe they are giving out. It doesn't matter if I like it or it works for me, if the kids don't find it authentic then they will let me know and I have to change it. Sometimes something doesn't work because I haven't modeled it enough. Sometimes it is because it isn't challenging them enough. Regardless, the goal is to be flexible but structured. I need the structure and so do the kids."

Classroom Management in the Vocabulary Classroom

According to Jensen (2009), the brains of babies are hardwired for only six emotions: joy, anger, surprise, disgust, sadness, and fear. All other responses to life situations, such as humility, forgiveness, empathy, patience, cooperation, and optimism, must be learned. Students being raised by caregivers who are young, inexperienced, or overwhelmed by the stresses of poverty may come to school with underdeveloped emotional responses. Consequently they may not be able to work as well in cooperative settings and they may not know how to react appropriately in social situations. As Jensen states, "Every proper response that you don't see at school is one you should be teaching." This includes modeling and practicing appropriate academic behavior as well as the social skills necessary to work as a team.

We won't pretend that everything goes smoothly in the beginning. Our students often have had to fight, both literally and figuratively, for what they need. Their spirit and resilience are admirable, but it's our job to help them channel their energy so they can be active and have fun with learning while developing self-control. With some groups of students this process takes longer than with others and usually depends on whether they have had teachers who use authentic discussions to boost language learning.

Our umbrella classroom rules are always "Be respectful, Be responsible, Be prepared." What that mantra looks like is actually up to the students. They brainstorm each rule and then decide as a group which qualities are most important. We display the rules on a chart, and everyone signs it like a contract.

We also model, model, and model again appropriate behavior. In the beginning of the year we will actually practice getting excited (laughing, jumping, you name it) and then calming down and refocusing. This process might sound silly, but it's necessary and it works. Our students need those fun times but they also need to learn how to not take exuberance too far so they can get back to work.

In addition, we celebrate when our students demonstrate self-control and self-reliance. The adults in our building are always on the lookout for outstanding examples of good behavior, kindness, and thoughtfulness and offer compliments when appropriate. Kudos can take the form of comments on small deeds, such as "Great line!" in the hallway. Maybe a student helped clean up in the cafeteria or offered encouraging words to someone. These acts of good citizenship are often noticed by others.

In both classrooms, a "compliment jar" sits on a table by the door. As students receive compliments from others around the school, they get to put marbles in the jar. Sometimes we will discuss a particular compliment as a class to decide if it is deserving of more than one marble. When the jar fills up, we hold a party on a Friday afternoon. We ask students to make suggestions for party themes, and then they vote. Sometimes they choose a popcorn party or a dance party to celebrate a job well done. Although some people may view this as extrinsic motivation, we understand that our students need tangible acknowledgments of their ability to conduct school business in a respectful and focused manner, which then carries over into all academic areas. When marbles mount in the jar, students feel very proud of themselves. We have *no* problem celebrating a jar full of awesome behavior!

Fostering Self-Reliance

When Margot and Leslie first began teaching, they set up their new classrooms and arranged materials to have everything they needed at their fingertips. At a faculty meeting during the beginning of their second year of teaching, their principal gave a three-minute talk that changed their thinking profoundly. Dr. Dewey Hensley challenged his teachers to look at their classrooms through their students' eyes. Were their classrooms teacher convenient or student convenient?

Margot says, "It wasn't until my principal explained the difference between the two types of classrooms that I even realized there *was* a difference."

Dr. Hensley stressed that in teacher-convenient classrooms the teachers organize materials that are easily accessible for adults, and materials are often not made available for students to use without permission. If materials are available for student use, then sometimes they are not clearly labeled, making it confusing for students to find the items necessary to complete work. In a teacher-convenient classroom the majority of the space belongs to the teacher, whereas in a student-convenient classroom a majority of the space belongs to the students. By contrast, in a student-convenient classroom the materials are purposeful and help students achieve optimal success.

Both Margot and Leslie took this lesson from their principal to heart. The faculty and staff at Atkinson strive for the school to be "poverty considerate," and creating a student-convenient classroom is an important step toward that goal.

Although Leslie and Margot share similar philosophies about teaching in general, and vocabulary instruction in particular, they have different personalities and ways of teaching. The following sections show how their classroom organization approaches reflect a contrast in styles. The important message is that structure and creativity are not mutually exclusive; they both play a vital role in learning.

Margot's Primary Classroom Space

When crossing the threshold into Margot's primary classroom, most people get a calming sense of order. Desks are clustered so that students can easily turn and talk to partners and engage in various group activities. Margot arranges her classroom into four groups of six desks. She has found that this organization works best because students can easily collaborate with one another at any moment.

The remainder of Margot's classroom is set up in sections according to content. For example, her classroom library is located in the northwest corner of the room. A brightly designed carpet makes a comfortable place for whole-group shared reading and chart instruction. A wooden rocking chair sits on one edge of the carpet, and shelves with baskets of books line two sides. Other reading materials, such as literacy anchor charts and bulletin boards, are also located in this general area of the room. Margot displays vocabulary anchor charts containing targeted vocabulary words and their synonyms and antonyms above the library (see Chapter 4 for vocabulary anchor charts).

An anchor chart is a visual aid (usually done on large chart paper) that we create during or immediately after instruction and display when the lesson ends. We want kids to have a way to remember their learning, so we use an anchor chart to help them ballast and further develop vocabulary concepts. Some teachers may wonder if the chart can be used to "cheat" when students are working. We actually encourage our students to use the chart for reference. We make each chart clear and plain, so it can be used as a reinforcement, not a distraction.

Three student computers are located in the northeast corner of the room, near the writing nook. Margot has placed benches there with plump cushions for students to sit on. Small bookshelves contain writing and reference materials for students to use.

Next to the student computers, on the east side of the room, is the guided reading area. A kidney-shaped table with five chairs sits in front of a bulletin board. All materials that are used during this time are located on a table next to the guided reading table, making the materials accessible to Margot and her students. Having the guided reading area in this position helps her see all students at all times while she is conducting small groups. She also uses this same area for guided math groups in the afternoons. There is a large bookcase located on the opposite side of the table that houses all the math materials so she and the students can get to them easily.

The west side of Margot's classroom, by the windows, is for Margot's desk and storage area. The south wall is dedicated to math, science, and social studies content anchor charts.

Margot's classroom works because she is organized and efficient, taking into account her students' needs. She has prepared her classroom materials, furniture, and supplies so that students can practice self-reliance. She has carefully planned her lessons and activities so that connections are obvious. Her students feel free to express their opinions, and she encourages them to try new things. Vocabulary learning flourishes in such an environment.

Leslie's Intermediate Classroom Space

Leslie's classroom is also organized, but the atmosphere is a bit more playful. There are plenty of places where students may go find a spot on the floor to work alone quietly, with a partner, or with a group. They often use beanbag chairs and throw pillows to stretch out on the floor. Leslie arranges the desks for easy collaboration, sometimes in groups of four or six, sometimes in a horseshoe formation, and sometimes in two groups to create two large tables. She always leaves the perimeter open around the desks so students can work.

Leslie's room is also student convenient. She always has paper, graphic organizers, pencils, and other supplies labeled and easily accessible. Although she had dreamed of having a classroom where buckets of supplies would sit in the middle of the tables, she soon realized that the dive for the purple crayon or pink highlighter was too distracting for her. So, instead, students have their own supply boxes, which include glue sticks, scissors, highlighters, crayons, and colored pencils, and Leslie replenishes these as needed. On one side of the room, a bookcase holds a class set of student dictionaries and thesauruses, which students use every day for vocabulary study. All reading anchor charts go on the east wall, and all math anchor charts go on the west wall. Vocabulary anchor charts go up in front so that kids can refer to them easily.

Leslie got rid of her own desk when she realized that she was just using it as a place to stack things. If she sits, she does so at the guided reading table or out at the desks with the kids. She wants students to be comfortable working in front of her. This way they are always used to her being "in the mix."

Everything in Leslie's classroom is a study in student independence. At the beginning of each school year she prints out a page of labels for each student. She asks the students to label everything with their names so they have ownership and are responsible for their materials. One student comes in every morning and sharpens a designated set of pencils that is available for the day. Other students tidy the room, help create anchor charts, and help prepare teaching materials for the group. Leslie wholeheartedly believes in kids feeling invested in their classrooms. She says, "Everything from classroom rules to placement of loose-leaf paper can be made by the students."

Leslie's classroom works because Leslie and her students trust each other. Leslie's classroom is relaxed, but high expectations are unmistakable. The classroom is student centered, and her students learn to be good citizens who help each other learn. Vocabulary development also thrives in this type of environment.

Vocabulary Development as Part of a Bigger Literacy Design

We know that vocabulary development does not and cannot exist in a vacuum. To achieve the goal of multiple exposures to words that build word schema, we have to emphasize vocabulary instruction throughout the curriculum and across the school day. However, we have found that dedicated time to vocabulary development is essential.

As teachers and teacher-educators who collaborate, we share a philosophy of comprehensive literacy instruction. In this type of classroom, the day includes a coordinated set of literacy experiences designed to help all students and address their different learning styles. Students are involved in shared reading, guided reading, word recognition instruction, writing, self-selected reading, and interactive read-alouds drawing from children's literature and interesting informational materials. We explicitly teach vocabulary during shared reading, but embed vocabulary instruction and experiences throughout the school day and into content-area instruction.

A schematic of our classroom literacy design might look like Figure 2.1.

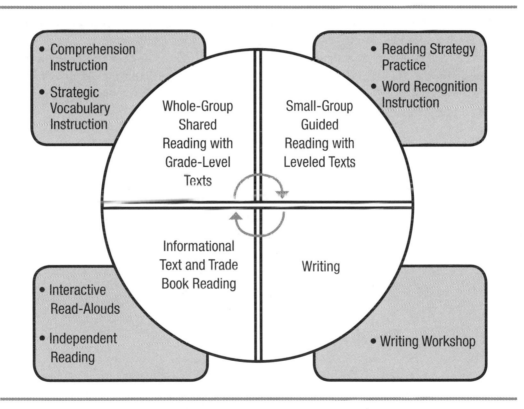

Figure 2.1 *A comprehensive literacy design to promote vocabulary development*

Whole-Group Shared Reading with Grade-Level Texts

In shared reading, the goal is to introduce comprehension skills and strategies to the entire class. Everyone has a copy of a text with the appropriate complexity for the grade level, or they can see the text on an electronic whiteboard or a chart. Shared reading is where we help our students learn to interpret text. This is also the time we teach explicit vocabulary lessons.

Small-Group Guided Reading with Leveled Texts

We group and regroup our students for guided reading based on assessment results. In guided reading, students practice the strategies they have been taught in shared reading, but use texts on their instructional level. We often reinforce vocabulary strategies in small guided reading groups.

Teaching word recognition is also part of guided reading groups. Because we work with older primary and intermediate students, we don't need to focus as much on basic phonics skills unless assessment results show that a group needs a certain word recognition skill. Mostly we teach students how to decode multisyllabic words as they encounter the terms in their leveled texts. They decode multisyllabic words by dividing them into syllables and pronouncing each syllable. As students learn to decode, we also discuss the meanings of prefixes, suffixes, and roots.

Writing Workshop

Writing workshop (Atwell 1987) is another part of our comprehensive literacy classroom design. In writing workshop, the teacher introduces a mini-lesson about a writing strategy, skill, or genre, and then students write, revise, edit, and share their writing. Students write every day. We analyze our students' writing not only for form and style, but also for vocabulary use, and we encourage kids to celebrate a classmate's use of amazing vocabulary in writing. This celebration often sparks more complex writing from other students in the class.

Trade Book Reading

A small but significant portion of the day is dedicated to experiences with trade book reading, children's literature that might be found in a good bookstore or a library. Sometimes we show the illustrations, and sometimes students just listen for the story, structure, and word use. We make sure there are plenty of read-aloud experiences with quality literature, both fiction and captivating, well-written informational texts. Read-alouds often connect to a theme in science, social studies, or math, but sometimes the only purpose of a certain read-aloud is to add an element of play with words.

Many of our students have little access to text outside the school day, so we try to ensure that they will always have books to take home with them. However, independent reading of self-selected texts in school is also an important part of strategic vocabulary instruction. We provide time for students to read a book of their choice and record their reflections in response journals. We then provide written feedback to students who point out notable words or use targeted vocabulary words in their reading responses.

The Daily Schedule

At Atkinson Academy, the principal begins each day with a twenty-minute, schoolwide meeting in the gym to help students shed the cares of neighborhood stresses, reestablish the school community, and get ready to learn. When Margot's primary students return to the classroom, a ninety-minute uninterrupted block of reading begins. Margot starts with a thirty-minute shared reading and vocabulary lesson and then transitions into small guided reading groups. Beginning with shared reading gives Margot an opportunity to model various comprehension strategies before students are released to apply those strategies independently. After shared reading, Margot meets with three guided reading groups for approximately twenty minutes each. While Margot meets with small groups, the rest of the students participate in independent work, such as vocabulary journals or writing, literacy centers, or self-selected reading with response journals.

In Leslie's classroom, students return from the schoolwide meeting to start on a daily oral language exercise she has prepared. Vocabulary and shared reading come next, lasting about an hour. Afterward, students go to their literature circles and work on portfolios or reader response journals, meet with their guided reading group for a performance assessment task, participate in reader's theater, or meet with Leslie for small-group instruction. She usually sees two groups a day for twenty-five minutes each, and then she conducts individual conferences for ten minutes at a time.

The first two days of direct vocabulary instruction usually take up the majority of shared reading time in the beginning of the year until students are familiar with the routines and procedures. Then the process moves more quickly. Occasionally vocabulary lessons extend beyond thirty minutes because rich class discussions or misconceptions mean we have more to talk about. When this happens, we adjust the schedule by meeting with two out of three groups during the guided reading time. Then we meet with the third group during a thirty-minute additional block of reading in the afternoon.

Academic Discussion

A key part of our vocabulary instruction is academic discussion. We include some of the Speaking and Listening standards from the Common Core State Standards in our vocabulary plan.

CCSS Speaking and Listening Standard 1 states that students will be able to "participate in collaborative conversations with diverse partners about [grade-appropriate] topics and texts with peers and adults in small and larger groups" in grades kindergarten through two and "engage effectively in a range of collaborative discussions (one-on-one, in groups, and teacher-led) with diverse partners on [grade-appropriate] topics and texts, building on others' ideas and expressing their own clearly" in grades three through five. Our strategic vocabulary instruction embeds varied opportunities for students to engage in collaborative discussions about words, texts, and ideas.

We begin with instructional conversation (Tharp and Gallimore 1991). We plan the topic but the students direct the discussion based on their questions, insights, and ideas. In instructional conversation, we carefully listen to students' comments and insert questions and comments to help push learning to new levels. (See Chapter 3 for more details about how academic discussion, based on the concept of instructional conversation, is part of introducing new vocabulary words in every vocabulary cycle.)

We also plan many opportunities for students to conduct academic conversations with peers. For example, we place students in mixed-ability groups and move them around as needed. Sometimes they might discuss topics with their "elbow partner." Other times they might work with the person across from them or with everyone at their table. In Leslie's class, all students have a Popsicle stick at their desks. The sticks are color coded, with a number on one end, a letter on the other end, and a symbol in the middle. Leslie may say, "Get with your 'A' group," or "move to your blue group." By using this method, students are always working with different groups and classmates. Leslie explains, "This *really* helps with classroom community. Everyone is included. Students have an ease with working and talking with each other. Sometimes it isn't a match made in heaven, but that's okay. It is good practice for them to work with someone they don't want to be friends with but affords them an opportunity to practice respectful behavior."

We also model different conversation styles so that students understand appropriate ways of working together. If a group is having problems, we might discuss the conflicts and brainstorm better ideas for cooperating. When we model decision-making for students we always list pros and cons of the various choices so they can consider the differences. Many examples of student-to-student academic discussions are included in the pages of this book.

Choosing Vocabulary Words

Choosing the right vocabulary words is usually challenging for teachers. Because there are so many thousands of words to choose from, we have to be strategic about narrowing our selections. Here are some options.

Choose Words from a Commercial Reading Program

We teach in a school that has a commercial program available to teach reading. Although we don't follow it precisely, and our principal encourages us to do what's best for the students in our classrooms, we choose many of the materials from the reading program. Each two-week science or social studies unit focuses on a specific comprehension strategy, using stories and passages that are related to a content area. For example, during the first two weeks of school third graders review how to make connections using passages that are related to social studies. During the next two weeks, they move on to asking questions using science-related passages, and so forth. Although strategies are introduced and practiced separately, we teach students to use a combined repertoire of strategies when they read. The commercial reading program also provides five content-area vocabulary words that should be taught for the first week and another five during the second week.

As our focus on vocabulary became more intentional and more activities evolved, we realized that five days was not enough to teach new words that students would remember. Children were not getting enough opportunities to interact with the words and practice using them in oral and written language. So we decided to move to a ten-day plan. We looked for relationships between Week One and Week Two words and discovered that some of the words could be used as synonyms and antonyms for one another and that there was no need to teach some words because our students already knew them.

Instead of trying to teach ten words every two weeks, we decided to begin teaching six of those ten words. We tried to choose a balance of Tier Two and Tier Three words (Beck, McKeown, and Kucan 2002). We particularly chose words that were content specific because we knew our students would encounter those words not only during reading, but also during science and social studies. We also chose words that were general in nature that our kids may not have heard before.

Choose Content-Area Words

Several years ago Brenda was leading a workshop with middle school teachers from nine different school districts. In Kentucky students are required to write short answers to extended response questions as part of the assessment in grades three through twelve, and these teachers said their students had performed poorly on the tests. The teachers were surprised and frustrated by the results because previous class work and practice tests had suggested that students knew the content covered on the exams.

"I know my kids! I know they know this stuff!" exclaimed Joe, a seventh-grade social studies teacher.

Heads nodded around the room, as other teachers agreed with his statement.

"Then why aren't they showing it on the test?" Brenda asked.

As a group, the teachers brainstormed possible reasons. Brenda encouraged them to think about student behaviors they had observed during the last test session.

"It's like some of them just quit trying in the middle of a question," sighed Margaret, a sixth-grade language arts teacher.

"Not just some of them. A *lot* of them," added Susan, a teacher of eighth-grade science.

"Why do you think that is?" Brenda asked.

After a moment, Joe quietly said, "Maybe they are shutting down because they don't know the vocabulary."

Immediately the other teachers caught fire with the same recognition. As they discussed the issue, many teachers acknowledged that they hadn't taught vocabulary explicitly or they had used less sophisticated words in class when the test required students to recognize and know appropriate subject-matter terms. No wonder students were shutting down on the exams! As a result of that workshop, Brenda and the teachers collaborated on a vocabulary list for each subject area and teachers learned new ways to teach vocabulary within content-area classes.

We believe that with the current emphasis on standardized testing, a healthy dose of content-area words should definitely be included in vocabulary study for any grade. We suggest reviewing upcoming themes and units in science, social studies, math, and the arts. Choose words that students will encounter often in their school careers. For example, a word such as *culture* shows up often in science, social studies, and popular media, so it would be an excellent choice for teaching multiple meanings of a word.

In the Common Core State Standards, Language Standard 6 sets the expectation that students will be able to accurately use grade-appropriate domain-specific words and phrases by grade three. This expectation has an added benefit. Once we started choosing subject-specific words for our strategic vocabulary instruction, we realized that our students immediately made stronger connections to science and social studies concepts. Extended experiences with words such as *organism, analyze, geology, consists, interaction, artificial, prey, adaptation, relocation, predator, solution,* and *nutrient* helped them build a background in science. Our students' social studies knowledge also grew by learning words such as *negotiate, sacrifice, fair, trade, wealth, foreign, canyon, perimeter, population, region, passage, voyage,* and *claimed.*

Choose Tier Two Words

Beck, McKeown, and Kucan (2002) recommend analyzing a text for Tier Two words that might be important for understanding the selection. These include words such as *hesitated, extraordinary*, and *slump*, which students might encounter in future texts or which will help them describe concepts. The authors suggest three criteria for selecting Tier Two words:

1. *Importance and utility*—Words that are characteristic of mature language users and appear frequently across a variety of domains.
2. *Instructional potential*—Words that students can use to build rich representations of concepts and apply to other situations.
3. *Conceptual understanding*—Words that students may understand generally, but that provide precision and specificity in describing a concept. (21)

Tier Two words will differ depending on students' backgrounds, interests, and outside experiences, as well as their assessment results. What words do students already know? What words will students consistently encounter in texts? What words do they need to know? We can choose only a few words to explicitly teach. What words are going to provide the most bang for the buck?

A Note About Vocabulary Lists

Vocabulary lists can be found everywhere. Type "vocabulary list" into an Internet search engine and you will find a multitude of websites featuring high-frequency words, sight words, grade-level lists, idioms to help English language learners, and lists to prepare students for the SAT or GRE exams. If you use a list, please make sure it is appropriate for your students. High-frequency and sight-word lists are usually not right for vocabulary study because students probably already know the meanings of these words or how to use them in everyday language. Some lists of Tier Two words or content-area words include terms students may not see in their reading. Research-based lists of vocabulary words (for example, see Fry 2004) are often helpful, but these lists need to be analyzed with the needs of particular students in mind. We need to teach "Goldilocks" vocabulary words—just right for the students in front of us.

Our Strategic Vocabulary Routine

Over time we established a routine for strategic vocabulary instruction. We use the term *vocabulary cycle* for the period of time we are working on a set of words. We think the word *unit* implies that there is an end. In our strategic plan, vocabulary instruction with a collection of words does not end. Words appear again throughout the year in games and quizzes so our kids can continue to make connections. For every vocabulary cycle, we choose the words we will explicitly emphasize during lessons. For each vocabulary word, we select a kid-friendly definition using simple, everyday language. We also select a sentence to introduce the word, two synonyms or examples of each word, two antonyms or non-examples, and a picture or image to represent the concept.

As we worked on our plan, we shared our ideas with Maria Carrico, a reading coach in our school district. Maria helped us organize the components into a template she calls the Vocabulary Planner. Figure 2.2 shows an example of a completed Vocabulary Planner using a leveled text called *The Animals' Wishes* (Thomason 2000), a Native American folktale included in the Rigby Literacy Series. (See Appendix A for a blank template of the Vocabulary Planner.)

After we analyze a text selection and choose the most appropriate words for our students, we use the Vocabulary Planner to outline our instructional goals. Websites such as yourdictionary.com or Answers.com provide easy-to-understand definitions, sentences, synonyms, and antonyms that can help us quickly and easily find the information we need. We find additional synonyms at Synonyms.com, which often also suggests an antonym for each word. Adding clip art to the "picture" column of the Vocabulary Planner, as shown in Figure 2.2, provides an easy-to-replicate image we can use to help students relate to the words. We keep an electronic file of each vocabulary cycle to have a starting place for the next school year.

After choosing the words, we use the following routine for teaching vocabulary (see Figure 2.3):

Step 1: Introduce the terms using a pocket chart, word cards, a cloze sentence with a blank where the word should go, and kid-friendly definitions on sentence strips. Ask students to predict the words, try out the words, and begin vocabulary journals.

Step 2: Add synonyms (or examples) and antonyms (or non-examples). Finish vocabulary journals.

Step 3: Practice using the words with whole-group and small-group activities. Practice applications of synonyms and antonyms with whole-group and small-group activities. This step can take several days of intentional experiences.

Step 4: Engage in a whole-group activity to celebrate vocabulary learning.

Step 5: Assess understanding using a teacher-created test that resembles a standardized test.

We base our vocabulary instruction on these five steps and add activities as appropriate. All the activities become integrated into our vocabulary routine.

Text: *The Animals' Wishes* (Thomason 2000)

Word	Kid-Friendly Definition	Sentence	Synonym(s) or Examples	Antonym(s) or Non-Examples	Picture	Idioms and/or Other Meanings
Interrupt Pages 9, 13, 20, 23	To stop someone from continuing what they are saying or doing by suddenly speaking to them, making a noise, etc.	Sorry to *interrupt*, but I need to ask you to come downstairs.	Stop Suspend	Continue Silence		
Avoid Page ?	To stay away from someone or something, or not use something	It is a good idea to *avoid* his example because he is always in trouble.	Dodge Evade	Follow Encounter		*Avoid* him like the plague.
Feature Page ?	A part of something that you notice because it seems important or interesting	A long trunk is a distinguishing *feature* of an elephant.	Trait Quality	Uniform Same		Feature film Featured speaker
Pierce Page /	To stab quickly	As I walked through the haunted house, a sudden scream *pierced* the silence, scaring me to death.	Puncture Stab	Plug Heal		I *pierced* the steak with my fork. My sister *pierced* her ear.
Murmur Page 16	To say something in a soft, quiet voice that is hard to hear clearly	The girl *murmured* something polite, and smiled when I gave her the cookie.	Whisper Mutter	Scream Yell	 Gee, this is hard	

Extra Word Definitions

Creatures Page 2	Anything that is living, such as an animal, fish, or insect (BUT NOT a plant)
Gently Pages 4, 12	In a gentle (easy) way
Powerful Page 18	Something or someone who is able to control or influence events or other people's actions OR having a strong effect on someone's feelings or opinions OR a powerful feeling or effect that is very strong or great
Smeared Page 19	To spread something on a surface in a careless or untidy way
Glides Page 23	Something that moves smoothly or quietly without effort
Beneath Page 24	Under something or in a lower position than something

Created by Maria Carrico

Figure 2.2 *Vocabulary Planner using a leveled text called* The Animals' Wishes (Thomason 2000)

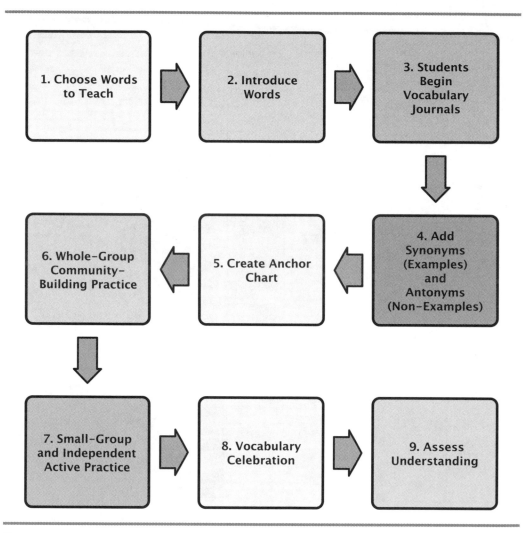

Figure 2.3 *Planning for direct teaching of vocabulary instruction*

Becoming Word Nerds

Planning a word-rich classroom means making sure the environment is conducive to vocabulary learning. In this type of student-centered environment, there is time to play with words and encouragement to do so. Direct vocabulary instruction is part of a comprehensive literacy framework, and vocabulary teaching is embedded across the school day. Teachers choose words carefully based on students' needs, and they make sure resources are at hand to foster student self-reliance. The ultimate goal for teachers is to develop the kind of environment that will help students become word confident.

Deyone demonstrated this confidence recently. During a science lesson the students were discussing how environments change. Ms. Lynd, the science lab teacher, explained, "Living things have three options. When their environment changes, living things can die, adapt, or move away."

Deyone raised his hand, and asked earnestly, "Ms. Lynd, shouldn't we really say, 'relocate' instead of, 'move away'?"

We cheer when we hear that our students have asked these types of questions! Words have power, and students who can use vocabulary appropriately and confidently are much more likely to be successful in school.

Chapter 3

Making Introductions

The beginning of wisdom is to call things by their right names.
—Chinese proverb

Students need time to explore new words, play with them, and connect them to concepts they already know. Words without a meaningful context remain random.

We consistently plan meaningful contexts for vocabulary study. We analyze the words we have chosen to introduce and think about how likely it is that students will encounter these words in their readings and assessments. We consider whether students may have background knowledge of the words.

According to Stahl and Nagy (2006), "Complex concepts require multidimensional teaching techniques" (77). Stahl and Nagy go on to say that to teach a concept, "one must (a) identify the critical attributes of the word, (b) give the category to which it belongs, (c) discuss examples of the word, and (d) discuss non-examples of the word" (77). Because of the time it takes to teach in such a deep way, Stahl and Nagy suggest choosing a few key words for such emphasis. In our classrooms, we introduce each word and then spend time examining the critical attributes, part of speech, examples, and non-examples. Our students require such deep context in order to learn new vocabulary.

We also try to make word learning a community experience and choose activities that will activate each student's word schema (Nagy and Scott 1990). This means providing opportunities for a variety of multisensory experiences and routine experiences with words. In addition, academic discussion, to varying degrees, is part of every lesson.

Vocabulary Learning in the Primary Grades

The words from the first week of vocabulary study are written on an anchor chart posted on the wall where students can see them at all times. For the second week of the vocabulary cycle, Margot has chosen five more Tier Two words—*anxiously, landform, breathe, architecture*, and *location*—that students will encounter in a reading selection.

1. Word Prediction

"It's time for vocabulary!" Margot says, and her students quickly gather on the carpet and look to the red pocket chart hanging from a metal stand. Margot has prepared three sentence strips in the pocket chart as a cloze activity, with a missing word in each sentence (see Figure 3.1).

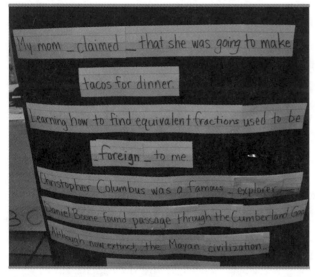

Figure 3.1 *Cloze activity used to introduce vocabulary words*

Cloze activities have been used to teach and test comprehension for years (Carr, Dewitz, and Patberg 1989; Chatel 2001). Cloze is based on the concept of closure, or the tendency to want to finish an unfinished sentence or text. For example, pretend that you are driving down the road listening to a favorite song in your CD player. When you stop the car and turn off the key before the song is finished, you may keep singing because you just can't help yourself. Most of us do that, at least when no one is watching. That's the cloze concept in action. In cloze sentences, the assumption is that readers must use context clues and inference skills to fill in a blank with a word that makes sense in the sentence.

The ability to "Use sentence-level context as a clue to the meaning of a word or phrase" starts at grade one in the Common Core State Standards (L.1.4a) and expands to the ability to use passage-level context in grade four. Margot uses a modified cloze procedure with her third graders to carefully introduce each vocabulary word in a way that allows students to play with inference and the use of sentence-level context clues.

Margot also has placed five index cards on the pocket chart. One side contains a vocabulary word and the other side a student-friendly definition. Margot will introduce three of the words on the first day and the other two words on the second day.

Margot picks up the first card with the word *anxiously*. She holds the card up in the air, making sure all the students on the carpet can easily see it. Margot chants, "My turn, *anxiously*. Your turn, _____."

Students fill in the word *anxiously* as they chant in unison.

Margot then claps the syllables as she slowly and carefully pronounces the word. "My turn, AN-CHUS-LEE. Your turn, _____."

Students imitate Margot, chanting the word and clapping the syllables.

"Now let's see if we can think about the meaning," Margot says. "Has anyone ever heard the word *anxiously*? What do you think it means?"

Students predict—some correctly, some incorrectly.

Sylvia tries it. "*Anxiously* means scared."

Anthony adds, "I heard that word before. I think it means being nervous."

Margot replies, "That's right, the word *anxiously* is an adverb. It tells how we might feel as we do something. It means to do something in a nervous, fearful, or excited way. Have you ever done something *anxiously*?" We let our students explore the meaning of the word before we tell them. If they are completely off track, we remind them to hold on, because context clues might help as we continue the word introduction. Now Margot calls on several children to describe when they did something anxiously or felt anxious.

Margot makes a conscious effort to teach the parts of speech as she introduces words because this is a skill that can help students figure out the meaning of words by the use of sentence structure (syntax) and context. We don't want our students to merely memorize words. Instead, we want them to learn strategies for word solving. By introducing words in a cloze format, students practice word solving by using both syntax and context clues.

Margot moves to the second word, which is *landform*, and then to the last word she will introduce on day one—*breathe*. After My Turn, Your Turn, she asks, "How many syllables does the word *breathe* have? The word *breathe* is a verb, an action word. *Breathe* is how air moves in and out of your mouth and nose—like your air tank."

Margot shows the students a "kid-friendly" definition (see Figure 3.2) of each word. She reads the definitions aloud to the students, and then they read them together in unison.

At the beginning of the year, the vocabulary development process is new and students' attention spans are short. Later in the term, Margot will spend more time exploring word connections and will add more intentional Tier Three science and social studies words to her lists. She will also talk more about parts of speech. For example:

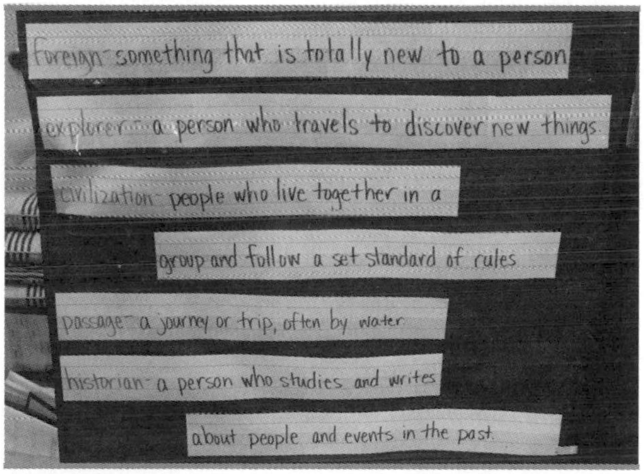

Figure 3.2 *Kid-friendly definitions for vocabulary words*

Margot: All right, the next word for this week is My Turn, *circuit*, Your Turn, *circuit*. My Turn (*clapping on each syllable*) SIR-CUT, Your Turn, SIR-CUT. All right, it has two syllables. A circuit is a noun, so it's a person, place, or thing. Typically it's a thing. What do you think a circuit is? Portia, do you want to take just a guess?

Portia: Something that can shut down.

Margot:	A circuit *can* shut down. Why would a circuit shut down? Ben?
Ben:	Because it gets too much electricity?
Margot:	Right, because it gets too much electricity. So all those appliances that you have at home and at school like our computers and things like that? Remember when all those wires were plugged up over here? That circuit was not getting enough electricity to make my computer work so my computer was about to shut down. If the lights start flickering in your house or the lights go out, it's probably because the circuit has shut down. It's the loss of electricity. So a circuit is a path through which electricity flows. Good job! That was a good prediction.

2. Trying Out the Words

From the first day of vocabulary instruction (and really, in all subject areas), we emphasize test-taking skills as we introduce words and help students complete the cloze activity. Test taking has recently been introduced as a genre (Kontovourki and Campis 2010/2011), and we now know that strategies that proficient readers use (asking questions; creating mental images; drawing inferences; synthesizing new ideas; activating, utilizing, and building background knowledge; determining the most important ideas and themes; and monitoring for meaning and problem solving) can improve students' test-taking skills (Conrad et al. 2008). We ask our students to use similar skills when deciding which word should fit into the blanks in each sentence. Although results are mixed about whether a cloze procedure can actually teach students to use inference and context clues when they are reading independently (Walters 2006), we think it enhances our students' ability to take a vocabulary assessment with cloze-like test items and thoroughly discuss vocabulary words and their meanings.

"Test makers try to trip you up," Margot tells her students. "You have to really use your context clues to figure out the right word."

In order for the cloze procedure to be effective in vocabulary instruction, sentences have to provide enough information for the students to be able to predict the meaning of the word that goes in the blank.

Margot and the students read the first sentence aloud together, saying, "blank" where the word is missing:

"Always remember to _____ properly while swimming."

Margot calls on a student to insert one of the three word cards into the sentences. "Amanda, can you put the word that goes into the first sentence in the pocket?" Amanda hesitates before picking up the card with the word *anxiously*. She inserts the card into the blank in the first sentence and steps to the side. Together, Margot and the students read the new sentence aloud.

"Always remember to *anxiously* properly while swimming."

Faces look puzzled and heads start shaking. Margot checks for individual understanding. "Okay, thumb up if you agree, thumb down if it doesn't make sense, thumb sideways if you're not sure."

This quick-response method helps us swiftly assess which students are developing an initial understanding of the words as well as correct any misconceptions. Such informal assessments also enable us to see which students are learning how to use thinking skills, such as using inference and context clues, to determine which word goes into the blank. If many students continue to struggle with making inferences and using context clues, then we will adjust the next day's lesson to include more practice. If only a few students are confused, then we will make adjustments during small-group instruction. The same holds true for students who are performing well during this activity. If a majority of the students seem to understand a word or understand how to use their context clues, we will increase the rigor of the lesson by challenging them to think of how the word could be used in a different context.

Students wiggle their thumbs in different directions; then gradually the majority of the thumbs point to the floor. "Great! You are really thinking! And Amanda, thank you for taking a risk." Amanda smiles and then sits down in her place on the carpet. Margot explains why the word *anxiously* could not be used in that particular sentence. She also asks students to explain what context clues from the sentence helped them make their decisions.

Margot places the same word card in each of the three sentence strips, following the same process as before. If the word fits, she still tries it in the other two sentences and asks the students to make sure. If students choose the incorrect word, she does not immediately correct them because students usually figure out the mistakes as they continue through the cloze activity. We want students to learn how to figure things out for themselves based on the information provided. We also want them to understand that even if one word seems right at first, another word may be a better choice so they need to try them all. Otherwise, many students will likely choose the first word without making a thoughtful choice that actually makes sense.

3. Primary Vocabulary Journals

Once Margot has introduced the first three words for the week, she asks her students to return to their seats and get out their journals. Students set off for their desks and pull out yellow folders with the words "Vocabulary Journal" printed on the front. At the beginning of the year, Margot prepared a folder for each student with a stack of graphic organizers inserted. The graphic organizer is a modified Frayer model (Frayer, Frederick, and Klausmeier 1969), which asks students to think about a word in several different ways. It is a simple square box divided into fourths, with a concept word in the middle where the smaller boxes intersect. In the top left-hand box, students write the definition of the concept word and in the top right-hand box they describe essential characteristics. The bottom left-hand box is where students list synonyms or examples of the word, and in the bottom right-hand box they place antonyms or non-examples. Higher-level thinking and word ownership are more likely to develop when students have to think of a non-example.

We have modified the Frayer model (see Figure 3.3) so that students can draw a picture in the top right-hand box to act as a logographic cue (Beers 2003). Creating a logograph, or picture that represents a concept, helps students internalize the meaning of the word within the context we have provided. (See Appendix B for a blank template of the adapted Frayer model.)

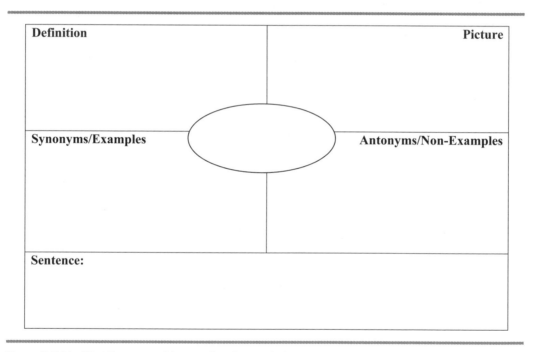

Figure 3.3 *Modified Frayer graphic organizer for vocabulary*

Margot always guides students in writing their vocabulary journals. Because her students come to school with many misconceptions, she makes sure that students are filling out the journals with accurate information. On this day, she uses a laptop connected to an LCD projector and projects the image of the Frayer model onto her whiteboard. Then, using the Windows Journal program on her tablet PC, she models how to fill out the vocabulary journal, color-coding the sections with her computer tools. (The same idea could be accomplished on an interactive whiteboard, wall chart, or overhead projector.) Students fill in the boxes in their own Frayer models as she does a think-aloud and completes the chart on the whiteboard.

Margot writes the word *anxiously* in red in the middle of her Frayer chart and then spells the word aloud. Together, Margot and her students add the correct part of speech, a student-friendly definition, and then draw a picture to help them remember the word. Next, Margot holds up a two-liter bottle of 7-Up and says, "Now I want you to write a 7-Up sentence!" Asking students to write a 7-Up sentence (Storm 2006) with at least seven words requires them to use adjectives, adverbs, and prepositional phrases in order to demonstrate concrete understanding of the meaning. There is some initial confusion ("Do you want us to write a sentence with seven words or add seven words?"), but students quickly get to work. Most begin with the sentence stem Margot has added to the bottom of the chart.

"Providing a sentence stem at first frees up space in their brains," Margot explains. "As the year progresses, I encourage them to create the entire sentence on their own. I always give them the opportunity to share their sentences as well."

Margot also creates the logograph for the top right-hand box. At the beginning of the year, she wants students to think about ways that logographs can be created to suggest the meaning of words. At first, many of the students copy Margot's drawing. When students are more independent, they create their own logographic representations of words.

Later in the year, completing the journal becomes an independent task once students have become familiar with the procedures and understand her expectations. As the students continue filling out their journals, Margot walks around the room and checks to make sure they are on track, another method of informal assessment. The synonym and antonym part of the chart will be completed on day two.

As students finish the first three words for the week, Margot takes a minute to do a quick review. "Who can tell me what the word *anxiously* means?" After asking two or three students to answer (and on day one, most students still have to look at their journal entries for what to say), she reviews the other two words and concludes the day's lesson by saying, "Wow! Give yourselves a big pat on the back!"

The completed journal is not graded; instead, students will use it as a vocabulary re-source. Margot wants the journals to be accurate, but she is more interested in ensuring that students can use the words correctly and become comfortable taking risks to try unfamiliar words (see Appendix C, "Vocabulary Journal Table of Contents").

Introducing New Words in Intermediate Grades

In the intermediate grades, we continue to introduce Tier Two words, but we also intention-ally focus on Tier Three, or domain-specific, words (Beck, McKeown, and Kucan 2002) as they are encountered in subject-area reading and discussion. Tier Three words, such as *isotope*, *peninsula*, and *equation*, are terms that students probably will not see in their everyday reading unless we specifically include them. Yet these words are vital to the comprehension of content-area concepts. In the Common Core State Standards, intermediate students are expected to "acquire and use accurately grade-appropriate general academic and domain-specific words and phrases" (Language Standard 6). Our vocabulary study at the intermediate level emphasizes academic and domain-specific words in order to build a strong framework for learning all content.

Let's take a peek into Leslie's fifth-grade classroom as she introduces six new words from a social studies text on explorers. Kentucky tests all fifth graders on their social studies knowledge, so Leslie makes sure to focus many vocabulary lessons on these terms. Leslie's word introduction has been expanded into four parts for her older students: Sentence Prediction, Word Prediction, Trying Out the Words, and Vocabulary Journals. Because students are familiar with the vocabulary routine at this point in the school year, she is able to introduce all six words on the first day.

1. Sentence Prediction

Leslie stands at the front of the classroom next to a pocket chart containing sentence strips—the same cloze-type activity Margot uses in third grade. However, on this chart the word cards are hidden. The students sit with their desks grouped together to form a horseshoe so all can see and feel part of the group. Anchor charts with words from previous weeks line the classroom walls.

"Let's see if we can make some predictions about our words," Leslie says. "See if you can use your context clues to predict what these words might be." She walks to the pocket chart and reads aloud from the first sentence strip.

There was a _____ of resources after Europeans came to America.

Hands shoot up as students start to hypothesize. The students sound as if they are asking questions, testing a possible answer, rather than deciding on a *Who Wants to Be a Millionaire*–type final answer.

"A speck?"

"A scarcity?"

"An amount?"

Occasionally, Leslie repeats the phrase so the student can hear if it sounds right ("a *speck* of resources?"). It is important to note that Leslie lets the students hypothesize and does not correct them as they practice using context to think about words that would fit. Right answers will come later.

The class moves to the next sentence. Leslie reads:

> *The Spanish explorers had _____ toward Native Americans.*

More students predict.
"Perceptions?"
"Traveled?"
"Issues?"

Students do not randomly guess, but instead try out words that they have heard or learned before that could be related to the sentence. In this way they "word-hypothesize" as they activate word schemas. This prediction skill is due to the strategy routine that Leslie has set. The students have participated in this activity every week to introduce their new words, and they are thoroughly familiar with Leslie's expectations.

On to sentence number three.

> *The _____ of America brought new people but moved many Native Americans from their homes.*

The students get into the spirit of the lesson and predict.
"Expedition?"
"Government?"
"Municipality?"
"Self-Govern?"
"Community?"

Students immediately see connections to words they have already learned. Although some of these answers could be wrong, Leslie smiles and verifies their predictions by saying, "I like how you all are using words from previous weeks!"

She moves on to sentences four, five, and six.

> *Buying meat and grain from farmers helps our _____.*
> *Columbus tried to _____ a route to Asia.*
> *There was a _____ between the conquistadors and the Native Americans.*

Students continue to hypothesize words that might make sense in the context of each sentence. Many are words they have learned previously but could make sense in the sentence.

Leslie continues to verify the quality of the students' predictions by saying, "Good words!" or "These predictions are awesome!" However, she still does not correct the students or give them the right answer. She merely allows them to explore the sentences.

2. Word Prediction

Leslie's enthusiasm for vocabulary is apparent as she moves on to the next part of the lesson and says, "Now let's take a look at these words and see if we can make some predictions about what they mean. I think you all are going to be really excited about a couple of them!" She holds up a card with the word *conflict* written on it. Like Margot, Leslie also does My Turn, Your Turn. She begins to embed instructional conversation about social studies concepts as she continues with Word Prediction.

Leslie:	My first word is *conflict*. My turn, CON-FLICT. Your turn . . .
Class:	CON-FLICT!
Leslie:	(*clapping the syllables*) My turn, CON-FLICT. Your turn . . .
Class:	(*clapping the syllables*) CON-FLICT!
Leslie:	How many syllables does *conflict* have?
Students:	Two!
Leslie:	What do you think this word means? Demetria?
Demetria:	A problem.

Other predictions follow.
"A battle?"
"An argument between two people?"
"Affect?"
"A war?"

Leslie allows the students to continue to predict the meaning of the word. Whether they realize it or not, as they predict they are connecting to the background knowledge generated in the first part of the lesson during Sentence Prediction as well as accessing their word schemas. Again, she does not tell them the right answer. This is time to explore by searching for meanings.

Leslie holds up another card with the word *prejudice* written on it. Leslie pronounces the word and does My Turn, Your Turn. Then she leads a discussion about the possible meaning. This time, Leslie draws students' attention to the use of morphological knowledge (the meanings of parts of words) to decide on the meanings of words in isolation.

Leslie:	What do you think *prejudice* means? Look at the first part of this word. What does *pre* mean?
Stacie:	Before.
Leslie:	Look at the root. What is the root word?
Stacie:	*Judge.*
Leslie:	Yes, so "to prejudge or judge before." What do you think that might mean?
Stacie:	To be mean.
Leslie:	To be mean?
Stacie:	To judge before you actually know.
Leslie:	So to judge before you actually know. Anyone else?
David:	To judge before judging.

Leslie also combines structural analysis (dividing words into prefixes, suffixes, and roots) with morphological knowledge to help determine a word's meaning. Leslie holds up the third word card. "All right! My next word is *colonization*." After another round of My Turn, Your Turn, Leslie says, "What do you think it means?" She points to the last syllable: "What does this part, the suffix, mean?"

Students	(*in unison*): The act or process of doing something.
Leslie:	Right! The act or process of doing something. So the act or process of . . .
Students:	Colonizing!
Leslie:	What is *colonize*?
Katlin:	Colonies?
Leslie:	That was one of our previous words. What does *colonies* mean?
Dante:	A community?
Leslie:	What kind of community?
Davion:	A settlement.
Leslie:	What kind of settlement?

Some students look through their vocabulary notebooks for the word *colonies*. One student reads from his notebook: "Oh! A settlement that is governed by someone from another place."

Leslie:	Mm hm. So . . . ? If a colony is a settlement that is governed by a king or queen or a government from overseas or from another place, what do you think the act or process of colonizing might be?
Tyrone:	Putting together a community?
Leslie:	The act of colonizing is starting a settlement that is governed by a king or queen. Right now we are talking about how the Spanish came over and started

settlements or colonies that were being governed by the Spanish monarchy. This is the act or process of colonizing. Who's doing the colonizing?

Katlin: Conquistadors.

Alexis: The monarchy.

Leslie: The conquistadors, the monarchy. Right now we are talking about the Spanish colonizing.

Students continue to connect their word schemas as they work on *economy* and *navigate*. Then Leslie moves on to the last word, which is *scarcity*. Students are getting excited as they connect this word to their sentence predictions. The student who had predicted *scarcity* sits up tall in his seat, knowing he got it!

3. Trying Out the Words

After leading student predictions for all six words, Leslie moves to the next part of the lesson by saying, "Okay, now let's see if we can figure out which words go where."

Leslie emphasizes test-taking skills during this part of the cloze activity. As Margot's third graders did, Leslie's fifth graders learn to try all the words in the sentence so they don't make a hasty and irrational choice. At the beginning of this part of the lesson, Leslie also reminds them to use the process of elimination by doing the *P-O-E* chant. This is a simple chant the students created as a class one day on the spur of the moment. Leslie said, "Good test takers and readers try all options first. We call that process of elimination—P-O-E!" A few girls added, "Oh! Oh!" to make it really rock. The whole class joined in and it became a chant. Leslie now can't say, "process of elimination" without the students breaking into the "P-O-E! Oh! Oh! P-O-E!" chant!

One by one, Leslie places each word card into the blank in each sentence so students can decide if the word would fit the context. Students call out an excited "Ding! Ding! Ding!" or a sad "Waa, waa, waa . . ." to mimic the sounds of a television game show as they indicate if they agree or disagree with the choice. Then they read it aloud together. If it makes sense, Leslie has taught them to use proper expression for the sentence. If it doesn't, their voices raise like a question (think "What????").

Leslie makes sure she tries each word in each sentence intentionally as this is a test-taking skill she wants them to know. She says, "I find that the best lessons occur when the kids are certain a word fits but then have to go back to adjust it because the remaining words don't fit the remaining sentences. This also is good test-taking practice because some answers are very close to being right but there is only *one* best answer."

As they work together to place the correct words in the card, Leslie uses this opportunity to also build more social studies background. Instead of just placing the word cards into the sentences, she facilitates a student discussion about the social studies concepts surrounding the word. By doing this, she helps cement the words into a word-schema network that students can access later.

Leslie returns to the first sentence and reads aloud the first sentence on the pocket chart. Students fill in the blanks and she helps them think about connections to their social studies work. Students often can be seen consulting their vocabulary journals for previous words, which is just fine with Leslie. Now *is* the time for right answers!

Leslie: There was a "blank" of resources after Europeans came to America.
Students: SCARCITY!
Leslie   (*putting the word card in the blank on the sentence strip*): "What kind of resources did they use up?"
Students: Jewels, buffalo . . .
Leslie   (*nodding*): Todd talked about that. Tell us what you said, Todd.
Todd   (*reading from his vocabulary journal*): "The Europeans started to hunt buffalo and they were dying off because they had no food."
Leslie: And were the Europeans hunting the buffalo for food?
Todd: They were hunting them for fun.
Leslie: And they weren't using all of the buffalo, were they? Sometimes they were just taking the skin and hides because that's what they could get money for, and then leaving their carcasses there to rot.

She leaves the word card that says *scarcity* in the sentence.

Sometimes students are not correct as they fill in the blanks. In that case, Leslie tries the card and they discuss it, but she does not leave it in the blank.

Leslie: The Spanish explorers had "blank" toward Native Americans. What do you think, Davion?
Davion: Conflict.

Leslie   (*putting the word card with* conflict *in the blank*): The Spanish explorers had conflict with the Native Americans? Okay, we'll come back to that.

She takes the card back out. Often, students become involved in a content discussion as they decide on the correct word.

Leslie: There was a "blank" between the conquistadors and the Native Americans.
Joanae: Prejudice.
Leslie   (*putting the word card in the blank*): We now have "prejudice."

Students:	No, that's not right.
Leslie:	Why not? There *was* prejudice.
Samuel:	I know! Conflict and prejudice are kind of alike.
Leslie:	Those sentences seem really similar, don't they? So that's why we're going to have to use our background knowledge to fill this in.

The conversation continues as the students discuss what they know about conquistadors, that they were warriors, which connects with the word *conflict*. The students then talk about the other types of explorers, missionaries, and noblemen. They brainstorm reasons that explorers might prejudge Native Americans. These opportunities for discussion are very valuable for content development.

The students' predictions of definitions are rarely on target when they begin this process. However, Leslie is amazed at how easily the students are able to use their context clues to decide which words go with which sentences. She says, "I think the part where the students make predictions about the definitions is a key component to this because it invites a dialogue to happen. This in turns creates safety, which becomes confidence in their ability. Combine that with the strategies for using the context clues provided and their background knowledge, and the results surprise and excite me almost every time!"

4. Intermediate Vocabulary Journals

Leslie's students also complete vocabulary journals, but they use a smaller, more compact version of the Frayer model graphic organizer to reflect their transition to the intermediate level. Leslie's intermediate students go right to work completing the organizer: filling in the word, simple definition, drawing a picture, and writing a 7-Up sentence.

After the class has completed the cloze activity, Leslie and the students add the words, definitions, and sentences to their vocabulary journals. She encourages her students to try their hand at creating their own sentences, but they are always welcome to add the sentence from the cloze activity. Students also draw pictures to go with their words. Again, Leslie encourages the students to produce their own pictures, but the words are still very new for them and it sometimes makes them feel more comfortable to be able to add the picture the class has used to go with the sentence from the cloze activity.

Extensions for English Language Learners

Our colleague Ashlee Kemper began her career at Atkinson but now works at another school in the vicinity. Ashlee was familiar with our strategic vocabulary instruction routine and adopted it for her second-grade students, about half of whom come from homes where Spanish is their first language.

Ashlee uses the same routine for introducing the words through a cloze procedure with a pocket chart and word cards. She involves students in academic conversations about the words that relate to their lives, and she also asks them to keep vocabulary journals. In addition, Ashlee makes sure that her students also know the vocabulary words in both English and Spanish.

At Leslie's suggestion, Ashlee adapted the Frayer model for her ELL students by adding a section at the bottom of the organizer to include a connection in their native language (see Appendix D). Because Ashlee is not a fluent Spanish speaker herself, she uses Google Translate (an app on her iPhone), to find the written translation and spoken pronunciation for her students. The students write each word in both English and Spanish, and her Spanish-speaking students write a sentence in English that helps them make a connection to the word. Ashlee then engages her students in the same types of activities that we describe in the rest of this book. The process has worked beautifully, and Ashlee and her students enjoy many of the same successes with vocabulary teaching and learning.

Investments in Vocabulary Building

Explicitly teaching vocabulary does take time, which might seem "expensive" in an already overloaded curriculum. As the examples from this chapter indicate, Margot and Leslie often invest whole-group reading instruction time to word study. But our experience and our students' test results have shown that building word schema and exploring word usage in this way pays off in the long run.

Naturally, the process takes much longer at the beginning of the year when students are first learning the routines. As the school year progresses, however, it takes less than half the time. Students can more easily use context clues and prediction to decide where the words in the cloze sentences should go and begin to apply the strategies independently.

Recall that Leslie's students had participated in the vocabulary routine before, so they began fifth grade ready to learn new words. Introducing the new words takes longer on the first day of the ten-day vocabulary cycle because Leslie also engages students in an in-depth discussion about vocabulary concepts, which helps increase their content knowledge foundation.

Keep in mind that many things are accomplished during word introduction! Students are examining prefixes, suffixes, and roots; identifying parts of speech; and connecting new vocabulary to previous terms. They are making inferences and using contextual clues. They are practicing test-taking strategies. They are having in-depth discussions about words that they will encounter in their readings. Literacy is alive in these classrooms, powered by a shared passion for vocabulary knowledge.

Chapter 4

Squeezing the Juicy Words—Adding Synonyms and Antonyms

The difference between the almost right word and the right word is really a large matter—it's the difference between the lightning bug and the lightning.
—Mark Twain

When we think about how our students must compete in the academic world with kids who have had so many more advantages, it reminds us of the Bob Thaves's quote about the 1930s movie star Ginger Rogers when compared with her dancing partner, the world famous Fred Astaire. "Sure he was great," said Thaves, "but don't forget that Ginger Rogers did everything he did, backwards . . . and in high heels."

Because many of our students come to us with basic or undeveloped vocabularies and with little word confidence, they often find themselves navigating the world of school talk in the manner of Ginger Rogers—having to work twice as hard to get the same results. The Common Core Standards expect all students to relate vocabulary to appropriate synonyms and antonyms by the end of grade four. Language Standard 4.5c states that students should be able to, "Demonstrate understanding of words by relating them to their opposites (antonyms) and to words with similar but not identical meanings (synonyms)." This is a sub-standard of Standard L.4.5, which says that students should "Demonstrate understanding of figurative language, word relationships, and nuances in word meanings."

Even before the Common Core Standards were published, we had taught our primary students, beginning in second grade, to find and teach their peers one or two synonyms and antonyms for each vocabulary word. When we cannot find a definitive synonym and/or antonym, we provide an example or non-example. This process increases the volume of words our students know. Adding synonyms and antonyms also enhances students' writing and oral language skills because they have more descriptive language at their disposal.

Research has found many benefits of including synonyms and antonyms in vocabulary instruction. In his extensive work on vocabulary development, Steven Stahl (1999) says teaching synonyms and antonyms helps students grasp a word's meaning. Stahl and William Nagy (2006), another well-known vocabulary scholar, stress that "Often, a synonym is all a person needs to understand a word in context" (64). Louisa Moats (1999) places vocabulary study squarely in the field of semantics, writing that words are learned in relation to other word meanings and that students should be able to "identify antonyms, synonyms, analogies, associative linkages; classes, properties, and examples of concepts; and denotative and connotative meanings" (25) in order to truly know a word. Moats also recommends including "context clues, semantic mapping and comparison, analogies, synonyms, antonyms, visual imagery, and other associations to teach meaning" (37). Camille Blachowicz, Peter Fisher, and Susan Watts-Taffe (2005) discuss the importance of teaching synonyms and antonyms to help students understand denotative (literal) and connotative (interpretive) meanings of words.

Using Reference Materials for Developing Word Relationships

The synonym and antonym step used to be our least favorite day of strategic vocabulary instruction because it seemed repetitive and a little humdrum. We would spend a lot of time finding the synonyms and antonyms we wanted to use in the lesson and then create a Word Document chart on the computer. We then devoted the second day of vocabulary instruction to introducing the synonyms and antonyms in much the same way we had introduced the vocabulary words the day before. Occasionally we asked students to brainstorm a synonym or antonym when we couldn't think of a good example. When students became comfortable with brainstorming, we showed them how to use the dictionary and thesaurus, the latter being particularly useful for learning synonyms and antonyms (Tompkins 2003). Students enjoyed this more sophisticated hunt for words, but we were still concerned that the process was too teacher directed.

One day Leslie was having a difficult time getting the computer to start so she could access the synonyms and antonyms she had chosen for her vocabulary study. After waiting a few restless moments for Leslie to get the technology under control, Daniel piped up, "Hey, Ms. Montgomery, why don't we just find our own words?" It was brilliant! With a nod from Leslie, two students passed out dictionaries and thesauruses. Leslie quickly arranged the students into groups of four and assigned them the task of finding appropriate synonyms for each word. The students immediately pulled out their vocabulary journals, opened the resource materials, and got to work.

As Leslie looked around the room, she was delighted. Every student was engaged and hard at work. Not only were kids practicing using the thesaurus and dictionaries but, once again, they were having a dialogue about words. The room buzzed as students found synonyms, discussed the choices with their groups, and decided on the best fit. When students review different definitions and discuss appropriate synonyms, they are learning that words can have multiple meanings (Mountain 2007).

Now, on the second day of every vocabulary cycle, students enter our classrooms and immediately head to the book shelf to find a thesaurus and search for synonyms and antonyms for the vocabulary words introduced the previous day (see Figure 4.1). This is a fairly informal activity; kids spontaneously form small groups or partners and get to work. As they discuss and debate, they make the words their own, as shown in this conversation:

Selena:	*Variety* means assortment. The synonyms are a *change*, *diversity*, or *difference*.
Paul:	Hmm, an antonym could be the same because it says it means difference.
Tionna:	Yeah, *same* would be the opposite.
Selena:	So we know one antonym is *same*.
Jermaine:	What's the opposite of *change*?
Paul:	If you got the synonyms, you can figure out the antonyms from the synonyms.
Jermaine:	I'm just trying to think of a good opposite of *change*.
Selena:	So based on our own definition, *assortment* is a synonym, maybe?

Later, the students search for synonyms and antonyms for *researcher*. The dictionary definition is "a scientist who devotes himself to research."

Selena:	Do any of you know what *devote* means?
Tionna:	I think . . . look it up.
Jermaine:	I think *devote* means when a person persuades themselves to do research.
Paul:	They don't got *researcher* in here (*looking in the thesaurus*).
Jermaine:	Try *research*.
Selena:	Here it is. "Analyze, experiment, investigation, study." Okay, we have to put our heads together. Let's just think a minute.

Figure 4.1 *DeEunique searches for synonyms in the thesaurus.*

Paul: So spell *research* and add *-er*.

Tionna: Analyze. Analyzer. Maybe *analyzer* can be a synonym.

Often the kids come up with much better words than we originally had planned to use because they can attach an experience to the word, either relating it to their own lives or to the small-group experience of finding the very best word. We see this activity as an extension of the Common Core Standards expectation, "Consult reference materials (e.g., dictionaries, glossaries, thesauruses), both print and digital, to find the pronunciation and determine or clarify the precise meaning of key words and phrases" (L.4.4c and L.5.4c) for fourth and fifth grades.

Finding appropriate antonyms can be challenging, so Leslie often offers teacher guidance. For example, when Leslie's class was working on a science theme about animals, she introduced *species* as one of the vocabulary words. When the class could not identify a good non-example for *species*, Leslie sent two students to the science lab to ask the science teacher. The students came back with the suggestion of *non-living*, which was ideal as a non-example. In science lab that week, the students categorized living, non-living, and once-living things—a perfect interdisciplinary connection.

We have used reference materials and websites such as www.antonyms.com to find antonyms, but student discussions usually promote greater understanding. Active participation in word study and discussions of words help with "depth of processing" and promote vocabulary learning (Carr and Wixson 1986).

After students decide on their antonyms, we ask them to share all the words they have found. We record their choices on a laptop and then project the list onto the whiteboard. A lively debate ensues as students vie to choose two synonyms and two antonyms for the final list. More dialogue about words, with students defending their choices! The class votes, and then we tag the winning words with a bullet point. Finally, the students add the words to their vocabulary journals (see Figures 4.2 and 4.3) while we complete a model on the laptop and project it for everyone to see.

Once students have completed their journals they help us make a class chart of the vocabulary words, using dry erase markers on a whiteboard (see Figure 4.4, page 58). The whiteboard chart includes each vocabulary word and the two synonyms and antonyms chosen by the class. Students create the whiteboard chart while we check to make sure the

Figure 4.2 *Shamyia works on her vocabulary journal.*

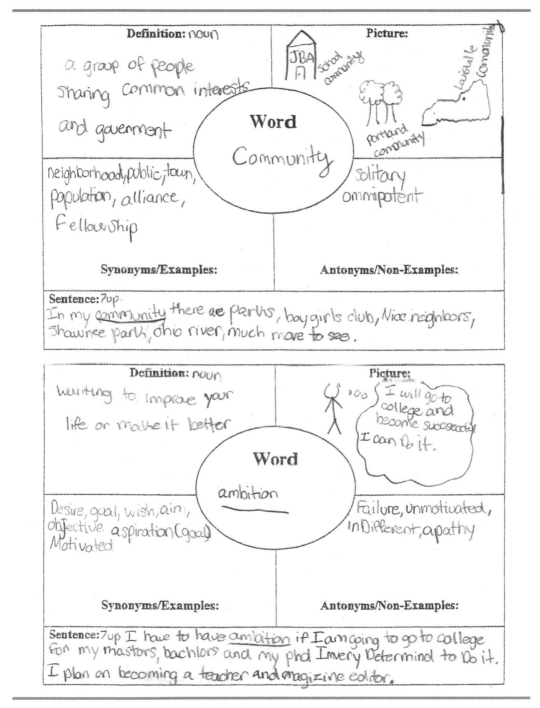

Figure 4.3 *A student's vocabulary journal entry*

Figure 4.4 *Zahria and Justice contribute to the class chart of vocabulary words on a whiteboard.*

words are spelled correctly and in the right places. The words on the whiteboard become a model for the rest of this vocabulary cycle, and the words get added to the anchor chart.

Teaching Tip

We encourage our students to use reference materials as part of our effort to promote independent learning. However, we always use the Vocabulary Planner (see Chapter 2 and Appendix A) to design our lessons even when the students find their own words. Sometimes the reference materials don't include the word, and sometimes the students don't choose the best words for the concepts they need to know. We like to have words preselected if students run into obstacles or misconceptions. The organizer helps us think through the lesson and be prepared.

Added Benefits of Vocabulary Research

Using the thesaurus to make class decisions on synonyms and antonyms has proved to be motivating to our more reluctant students. For example, D.J. was a small, shy boy who rarely spoke in class discussions without teacher encouragement. One day, as D.J. searched the thesaurus for a synonym for *belief*, he came across *conviction*. When Leslie asked for the synonyms the students had discovered, D.J. raised his hand and contributed *conviction* to the class list. His peers later chose his word to be an official class synonym, and D.J.'s chest puffed with pride. He definitely had "conviction" that his classroom contributions were valued.

Learning to use a thesaurus also opens a multitude of vocabulary learning and problem-solving opportunities. One day, Alexis skipped up to Leslie and exclaimed, "Ms. Montgomery! We couldn't find the word *germinate* in the thesaurus, so we did it another way. We figured out that *germinate* means 'to grow' so we looked up *grow* instead!"

Leslie said, "Wow! Thanks for sharing that with me. Can you go share with the other three groups who are still trying to find *germinate* in the thesaurus? Maybe you can give them a little direction."

"Sure!" replied Alexis, and relayed her group's newfound information.

This is the kind of conversation we long for our students to have. We want them to be able to dig deeper, to think of connections, and find alternate ways to explore words. We want them to understand how to use many tools to increase their word confidence and skills.

Velcro and Juicy Words

When our students first begin using reference materials to find synonyms and antonyms for their vocabulary words, they tend to choose words they already know. This is understandable—our kids have often been academic outsiders and naturally cling to the safest choices. So we nudge them toward more challenging terms by asking them to look for "Velcro words," the ones that will really stick to their brains. Gradually, as they get more used to vocabulary study, they become eager to find unusual words.

One day, as we were searching for synonyms and antonyms, Tayaunna found the word *melodious* and exclaimed, "Look at this word! It's downright juicy!" From that day on, our kids started calling an impressive synonym or antonym a "juicy" word.

Our students love looking up new and juicy words in the thesaurus. They have conversations about the meanings of the word, the way the words are pronounced, where or when they may have heard that word before, and what word it rhymes with or sounds like. We catch them using the juiciest words in everyday conversations. The week the students chose *immutable* as a synonym for *permanent*, Leslie overheard one student tell another, "The book fell behind the cabinet, but I can't get to it because the cabinet is immutable."

Our students become quite passionate about the words they find and delight in seeing new words in their texts. Without fail, our kids act surprised when they see a word they have recently learned. They sometimes get so excited that they will interrupt to make sure we see the words too. We decided long ago that no matter how annoyed we might feel when they interrupt during a math or social studies lesson, we will not show our displeasure. We want to share their excitement for word study. The kids have a sense that their new vocabulary learning is important and they need us to validate this for them.

One day Leslie's fifth graders were searching for synonyms for *nomadic*. Using the thesaurus, the students discovered *peripatetic*, a word not often found in elementary texts. Students declared peripatetic a "really cool, juicy word" and begged to use it for one of their synonyms.

Leslie acknowledges, "I honestly had never even heard of the word myself. So we looked it up in the dictionary to make sure it fit with our definition of *nomadic*. The kids really wanted to use that word. It was a challenge. They liked it. So we went with it and I have to say even I feel pretty cool when I use the word."

The fifth graders spent the next few days using *peripatetic* at every opportunity—in the classroom, in the cafeteria, and by all reports, at home as well. Not long after this incident, Brenda read in an article that in countries such as England and the Caribbean islands a teacher who travels from school to school to teach special subjects is called a "Peripatetic Teacher." Of course, the students were thrilled when she shared this information. The message: Juicy words can be found everywhere!

Vocabulary Code-Switching

At a session we presented at the Kentucky Reading Association conference, we shared our students' love of juicy synonyms and antonyms and most of the audience seemed impressed that they would use a word like *peripatetic* in conversation. However, a woman near the back raised her hand to make a comment. "This sounds great," she said, "but really, if we heard an adult using these kinds of words in everyday language we would say that person was acting like a jerk!" The audience laughed, but in all seriousness, she raises a good point. Our students love to play with words in the classroom and in school, but we always have to talk with them about the importance of code-switching.

Code-switching is the art of knowing when and how to use certain kinds of talk. Most people are fairly adept at code-switching when speaking to different listeners; after all, we don't usually employ the same language and manner of speaking at a football game that we do at a graduate seminar. Presidential candidates have to be masters at code-switching in order to appeal to audiences in varied communities (think about the difference in the manner in which politicians talk: folksy candidate speech in Iowa, sound bites when discussing an issue in New York City, and formal rhetoric when delivering a State of the Union Address). Being able to shift between dialects such as African American Vernacular English (Rickford and Rickford 2000) to Standard English, or being able to transition from English used in school to a Spanish discussion in one's Puerto Rican neighborhood, are examples of the ability to code switch.

Our kids become so excited about new words that they want to share their new knowledge with everyone. We worry (and sadly, it has happened) that they may be ridiculed at home or in their neighborhood for "showing off" their expanding vocabulary. This is why the classroom must be a safe place for students to practice their new learning.

We discuss where and when it is appropriate to use different types of talk and vocabulary. We make distinctions between what we call "Backyard Barbecue Talk"—the kind of pragmatic and casual conversation that is perfectly acceptable at a family reunion or at home with your friends—and "Professional Talk"—the kind of words you use in a discussion in the elementary classroom, at college, or on the job. By teaching our students how to gauge when each type of talk is suitable, we give them the confidence to hold their own in professional settings and the poise to participate easily in Backyard Barbecue Talk with their family and friends. We strive for culturally responsive teaching that is sensitive and accepting of home dialect and culture, but with the understanding that students have to learn the dominant code in order to take advantage of opportunities in society (Delpit 1995; Hill 2009; Ladson-Billings 1995; Lovelace and Stewart 2009).

Although we have limited family involvement at our school, the parents we have talked with have been happy that their children are learning vocabulary they may not know themselves. We regularly send home a brief classroom newsletter that contains a list of the vocabulary words we're learning. Occasionally students tell us that they and a family member study new terms together.

It's true that many people may not use words like *peripatetic* or *immutable* in everyday conversations. But how often are these types of words found on an SAT test or in a college lecture? We applaud juicy words. Knowing them will help our kids become ready for college and careers.

Going Deeper with Examples and Non-Examples

We have found that our students must spend time thinking deeply about both examples and non-examples in order to recognize appropriate word relationships. Even when a word does not have an obvious antonym, we still discuss non-examples of the word so they can grasp distinctions. William Powell (1986) finds that teaching polarity, or opposites, is one of the most powerful tools in vocabulary instruction, and Steven Stahl and William Nagy (2006) also discuss the benefits of asking students to contemplate opposites of vocabulary words. These researchers suggest that as students discuss what a word is not, they build deeper conceptual knowledge of what the word is. As Stahl and Nagy (2006) write, "We find that, even in less extensive vocabulary instruction, having children come up with antonyms (even for words without obvious antonyms) is useful in getting children to think about the meanings of words" (80).

For instance, students in Margot's classroom were having a discussion about the word *transit*. Shannon said, "An example of transit would be a car because it gets people from one place to another." Phillip responded by clarifying the comparison Shannon had made. "A car does get people from one place to another," he said, "but it can't take a whole lot of people somewhere at once. A transit is something that can take a lot of people from place to place like a train or a subway. Cars, bicycles, and motorcycles can only take a few people at a time."

Phillip's precise and elaborated description reflected his knowledge of the nuances of the word. Because our vocabulary study regularly includes examples and non-examples, students learn to parse terms for gradient meanings. Our kids don't become vocabulary experts over-night, but the more we practice the better they get at refining their word choices.

In the Common Core State Standards the ability to "demonstrate understanding of frequently occurring verbs and adjectives by relating them to their opposites (antonyms)" begins in kindergarten (L.K.5b). Although Stahl and Nagy (2006) caution against overdoing the teaching of synonyms and antonyms (especially antonyms for English language learners, who may become more easily confused), they also explain that the concept of adding syn-onyms and antonyms to vocabulary instruction can help cement word learning.

Word schema is further developed when students engage in activities that build syn-onym and antonym knowledge. When students learn how words are related, they have an easier time understanding nuances in meaning and how words can be synonyms and ant-onyms for other words. This knowledge increases students' conceptual word schemas, which is particularly important for children who have fewer experiences with academic language.

Beyond Synonyms and Antonyms

Usually on the second day of a vocabulary cycle, we ask students to find at least two syn-onyms, or examples, and antonyms, or non-examples, of each vocabulary word. We delib-erately choose vocabulary words we think students may have encountered or those that will extend a particular concept. Later, when students have more experience, we will scaffold our instruction so that they are doing more independent thinking.

The Setup in Primary Grades

For this vocabulary cycle, Margot previously introduced five new words—*coast, popular, distinguished, creek,* and *voyage.* She used a pocket-chart cloze-sentence exercise to initiate the study, and then she engaged her third graders in a collaborative academic discussion, helping them relate the words to their own background knowledge and experiences. Now it is time to explore word relationships and word schemas by adding synonyms/examples and antonyms/non-examples to the vocabulary unit. Although some of the words Margot has chosen for this lesson do not have obvious antonyms, she has thought about how she will lead students to consider non-examples for each one. As research shows, when students search for antonyms or non-examples, even when the word doesn't have an antonym, they build more conceptual knowledge about what a word means (Stahl and Nagy 2006). We engage students in exploring non-examples of words to help deepen their thinking about words. For instance, when students were searching for a non-example for *population,* they mused that the opposite of *population* might be *alone* or *solitary.* In turn, that led them to the word *extinct,* which they explained as "no population."

Margot begins this lesson on synonyms and antonyms by asking her primary students to get out their vocabulary journals. She has prepared a three-column chart on a mobile whiteboard. She labels three columns as Vocabulary Word, Synonyms, and Antonyms (see Figure 4.5; a blank template is available in Appendix E). She always uses blue for the Vocabulary Word column, green for the Synonyms column, and red for Antonyms. The color choices aren't important. The point is to be consistent because students make visual cues and connections to the color coding.

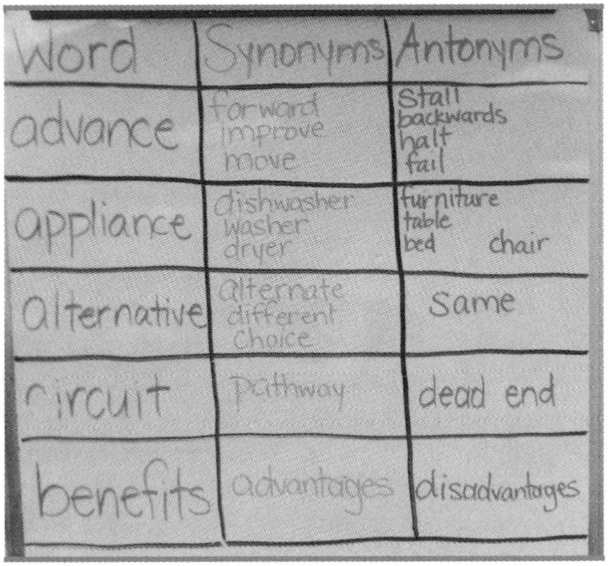

Figure 4.5 *Three-column word chart*

"Today, boys and girls, we are going to learn some words that will help us learn our vocabulary words," Margot says. "Our first vocabulary word is *coast*. Please check your vocabulary journals and see if you can tell me the definition of the word *coast*."

Margot carefully watches the class to gauge their ease with this task. Hands go up all over the classroom. Margot calls on William, a boy sitting near the back. "*Coast* means land that borders a body of water," William announces as he checks his vocabulary journal.

"Right," answers Margot. She pushes a button on her laptop and projects the Frayer model graphic organizer onto the electronic whiteboard (see an example of a Frayer model in Figure 4.6). "When we talked about the word *coast* yesterday, we said it was a noun—a thing. We said that *coast* was the edge of a big piece of land beside a body of water. We saw a coast on a map when we see the edge of land beside the ocean. We drew a picture of a coast next to water."

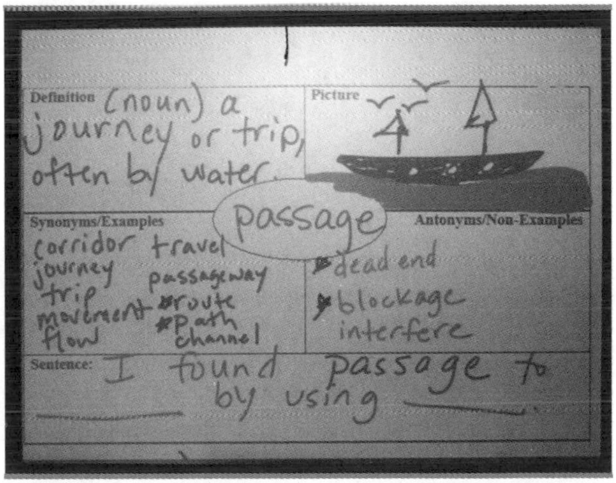

Heads nod; they are with her so far.

Margot continues, "Could a street be a coast? Could our school be a coast?"

Although most adults would understand that a street and a school could never be an example of a *coast*, such distinctions

Figure 4.6 *Example of completed Frayer model on electronic whiteboard*

are not always clear to our students. When students come to us with limited academic vocabulary, they also come to us with weak background knowledge. Often when our students learn something new, they are so excited that they attach the concept to things that are most familiar to them. In minds of some children, a street and a school *could* be a coast because both things run along the edge of something else. We have to engage them in discussions of what the word is *not* to help them truly understand what it *is*. Otherwise, we may have students pointing out the "coast" of the rug in the classroom! Because we know our students' tendencies, we can make sure that our lessons include visual models, virtual field trips, dramatic interpretations, stories from our own life experiences, and other sensory comparisons that will clear up confusion about new vocabulary.

Margot uses questioning and discussion until she is satisfied that her students have a good grasp of the meanings of the words. Then she introduces the antonyms she wants the students to learn and writes those under the appropriate columns on a whiteboard chart. The whiteboard will be displayed in the classroom throughout the vocabulary cycle, and then the words will be transferred to an anchor chart that will be posted on the wall as a reference for the remainder of the school year (see Figure 4.7).

Figure 4.7 *Vocabulary anchor chart*

Margot and the class work through the rest of the words. For *popular*, she suggests the synonyms *common* and *likeable* and the antonyms *uncommon* and *unlikeable*. For *distinguished*, students learn the synonyms *separate* and *set apart* and the non-examples *together* and *same*. On this day Margot chooses not to raise the extra complication of the word *distinguished* also meaning *admired* or *respected* because the text the students would be reading used the word *distinguished* as a verb, as in "distinguished between the two."

When Margot comes to *creek,* one of her students has a question that a child growing up in a rural area may never ask (further evidence that vocabulary words for one group of kids will not necessarily be appropriate for another). "Does a creek mean the same as a puddle?" asks Tyvon. Margot explains that a puddle comes with rain and dries up quickly when the rain is over. A creek is a continuous flow of water—it usually doesn't stop. Satisfied, Tyvon settles back into writing synonyms and antonyms in his vocabulary journal.

As Margot reviews the word *voyage*, she realizes that some of the students are still confused, so she demonstrates on the globe feature of the electronic whiteboard. "An expedition across the Atlantic Ocean to Africa is a voyage. An expedition across the Pacific Ocean to Japan is a voyage. *Expedition* means a long trip that is an adventure and is a synonym for the word *voyage*, except *voyage* usually means across water. Would an expedition from here to San Francisco be a voyage?" she asks, pointing to the West Coast of the United States on a map. As the students shake their heads, she says, "Another synonym for *voyage* is the word *journey*." Once Margot believes that the students understand the basic differences among *voyage*, *expedition*, and *journey*, she introduces antonyms for the words.

Vocabulary Lanyards

As part of our vocabulary study, we ask each child to wear a vocabulary word, synonym, or antonym on a lanyard—a fabric necklace with a clear plastic case clipped on to the end (see Figure 4.8). Students receive a different word each day, but we may also ask them to switch words during the day. This helps students realize that they must be responsible for all the words in this vocabulary cycle, not just the ones they may be wearing at the time.

As you will see in the following chapters, vocabulary lanyards become the basis of many review and practice activities.

Figure 4.8 *Students show off their vocabulary lanyards.*

Primary Grades Lanyards

Younger students wear their lanyards in the classroom, in the hallway, to special areas, and to lunch. We model and teach them not to pull on or twist the lanyard (and to ensure safety, we use the breakaway kind so students cannot choke on them).

Throughout the day we use the lanyards to place students in line. For instance, we might say, "If you are wearing the word that means _____, then line up here. If you are wearing the word that means the same as the word that means _____, then line up here. If you are wearing the word that means the opposite of the word that means _____, then line up here." We use this same method to call students to the carpet for whole-group activities. Randomly throughout the day we may say, "If you are wearing the word that means _____, then switch with the word that means the opposite of the word that means _____." A quick way to do this activity is just to ask all the words in a certain word entourage to line up.

We sometimes ask students to use their words in a sentence before entering and leaving the classroom. Other school employees in the building know about the vocabulary focus, and they may ask students to use their word in a sentence as the kids walk down the hallway, wait in the lunch line (we teach students to turn the lanyards around and put them over their shoulders as they eat lunch so that the lanyards stay clean), or go to special-area classes. We don't want students to be caught off guard and scared, so we make sure they have an opportunity to consult their journals when they receive a new word. If students are struggling, we allow them to write a definition and/or sentence on a card so they can remind themselves.

Students really enjoy these activities because they are aware that at any moment they must be ready to use their word correctly in a sentence or give information about their word. It holds them accountable and challenges them to constantly be thinking of the words for the week.

Intermediate Grades Lanyards

In the intermediate classrooms, we ask students to consult their vocabulary journals to make their own cards for the lanyards. If there are extra words, a student may wear more than one lanyard with synonyms or antonyms of the vocabulary words. After giving students a few minutes to use their vocabulary journals to review, we call up word entourages to fill out the chart together, listing the related words.

Intermediate students are more than willing to wear their lanyards in the classroom, but by about the middle of fifth grade they begin to balk at wearing them outside. That's okay with us. We will help them preserve their dignity, but inside the classroom active vocabulary practice continues.

The Magical Multiplication of Synonyms and Antonyms

One day in mid-January, when the temperature had dipped below freezing, Margot said, "Let's have a little quiz on synonyms." No one looked worried or even concerned; they had seen the glimmer of a smile on her face that meant this was going to be a fun activity. One student gave a little fist pump as his peers sat up straight and prepared to listen. Margot passed out a copy of a paragraph she had written for her students and read it aloud:

Greetings Earthlings! My name is Zapphorous and I am from the far, faraway planet known as Xenon. I have been on your planet about six months now. More specifically, I have been "spying" on your classroom for about two weeks! I must say you all are using some very unfamiliar words when you speak. I never heard such nonsense! I had a chat with your teacher and, boy, was it difficult because she was using the same words as you all. She explained to me that she has been teaching you new vocabulary words since the beginning of the year. Something about how it's going to help you become a better reader. Well, I don't believe it one bit! If you think you're so tough and know so many words, then let's play a game called "Crack the Code!" Here are the rules—I have written sentences in MY language. Your mission is to rewrite my sentences in YOUR language. There's a catch, however—you CANNOT use any vocabulary words to replace any of my words. You must only use synonyms. Make sure you use the CORRECT synonym! Do you think you're up for the challenge? Good luck and I will check back in with you soon! It sure is cold where you live!

After she finished reading the paragraph, Margot asked, "Do you think you are up for the synonym challenge?" The third graders nodded and smiled in agreement.

Margot read the first sentence aloud: *The meteorologist where I live never forecasts wintry weather.* She said to the class, "What is the vocabulary word in that sentence?"

Eight hands quickly shot into the air. David exclaimed, "*Forecasts!*"

"Great! You got the word!" said Margot. She then said, "What is a synonym for *forecasts?* Jodesha?"

Jodesha answered without hesitation, "*Predicts.*"

Margot read the sentence aloud with Jodesha's synonym: *The meteorologist where I live never predicts wintry weather.*

Margot then said, "Thumbs up if you agree." About half the students in the room pointed their thumbs up. The other half pointed their thumbs down or looked a little confused.

After a discussion about the meaning of *forecasts* and *predicts*, Margot wrote the sentence on the whiteboard, using *predicts.*

Matthew, who had his thumb down, spoke up. "Ms. Holmes, the reason I disagree is that I think it could be *projects.*" He pronounces the word with the stress on the second syllable.

Margot considered this. "Well, does it mean the same?" She read the new sentence aloud: *The meteorologist where I live never projects wintry weather.* "Which sounds better?"

A spirited discussion ensued. The class eventually agreed that *projects* could work, but *predicts* probably sounds more like what a meteorologist would say on a newscast.

Margot caught Matthew's eye and said, "Excellent thinking, Matthew."

Matthew exclaimed confidently to himself, "Yes! I am the *master* of synonyms and antonyms!"

The students wrote the new sentence on their paper, using *predicts*. They then turned to the next sentence: *I'm having trouble installing a Martian pool in my backyard because I do not have accurate measurements.*

The class decided the synonym for *accurate* was *precise* and wrote the new sentence. Then Margot asked the students to complete the rest of the sentences at their tables in small groups. The task was to choose the best synonym for the vocabulary word in the sentence and be able to justify the choice. Within seconds, the students were totally engaged in problem-solving their synonym word choices for each sentence.

Sentence number four was: *When I arrived on your planet I had to show a lot of caution because I was unfamiliar with the surroundings.* The vocabulary word was *caution*. Matthew's group decided to use *careful* in the sentence.

Matthew called Margot over to the table. "Wouldn't we need to say *carefulness* here instead?"

Margot replied, "Yes, you would need to add that suffix. Wow, you really took your smart-tee-o's today!"

One of the students in the group gave Matthew an admiring look. "You really *are* the best!"

Building Vocabulary Networks

Adding synonyms and antonyms to vocabulary study is a little like magic. We begin with one word, and by adding two synonyms and two antonyms for each, students suddenly know five new words. Five words each vocabulary cycle grows to twenty-five total words when we count up the synonyms and antonyms. Just like that, students' word banks grow and grow.

In reality, of course, it is not magic. It is intentional teaching. When we introduce synonyms and antonyms, we help our students build word relationships and vocabulary networks. Activities that require them to contemplate word meanings and engage in academic discussions about vocabulary enable them to construct deeper content knowledge, which in turn leads to higher achievement. Their success inspires them to learn more.

Chapter 5

Active Vocabulary Practice

Knowing more words makes me feel smarter. It gets the synapses going in my brain.
—David, fifth grader

We can probably all remember music or art lessons, sports activities, or hobbies we pursued in childhood. Whatever the new learning, we had to try out techniques, develop skills, and perform in authentic situations in order to improve. Few of us become competent without practice.

Motivation plays a big part in our eventual success as learners. Brenda vividly recalls taking piano lessons while in fifth grade. "You must practice, practice, practice," Mrs. White said after every lesson. "I can tell when you do not practice!"

Just *telling* Brenda to practice didn't make it happen, however. The isolated, unheated garage where the family's old piano sat was not a place that inspired devotion to music. Brenda did not practice, she did not get better, and she had no motivation to try.

As teachers we must remember that while we have had years of successful practice with academic vocabulary, most of our students have not had those same experiences. It is never enough to merely introduce words with their synonyms and antonyms and expect students to absorb them. We have to establish an environment that builds enthusiasm for learning and helps students develop confidence and competence with words.

Research shows that the human brain responds to unique experiences and that novelty causes a number of brain systems to become activated (Cell Press 2006). Michael Coyne and his colleagues (Coyne, McCoach, and Kapp 2007) find that providing "interactive opportunities to process word meanings at a deeper and more refined level," including discussing "target words in varied contexts," improves vocabulary learning for high-risk students (77). However, a constant stream of unrelated experiences is just as likely to cause confusion for students.

As we discussed in Chapter 1, our strategic vocabulary plan is loosely based on Marzano's (2009) vocabulary instruction model. One step of that instruction model is practicing new words in a variety of settings. Our students love to act, draw, sing, and talk, and they thrive when they are engaged in active learning. We rotate different types of practice activities during each vocabulary cycle, but we also stick to a routine that gives students emotional support and keeps practice focused.

Whole-Group Practice

Anyone who has been part of a team understands the benefits of working together to achieve an objective. According to the online Business Dictionary at www.businessdictionary.com, "A team becomes more than just a collection of people when a strong sense of mutual commitment creates synergy, thus generating performance greater than the sum of the performance of its individual members."

We think this is a good description of what happens when a group of students are engaged in learning and practicing vocabulary together. Acting as a team helps build classroom community and promotes positive academic risk taking. Students who are part of a vocabulary community get excited about words and want to make them their own. They help each other learn and cheer each other on. It becomes socially acceptable to achieve academic success.

In whole-group practice activities, we never miss a chance to help our students learn cooperation, patience, and empathy for others and further develop their social prowess while practicing vocabulary. Throughout this chapter we will share activities that have been particularly effective in reinforcing teamwork and vocabulary development.

Scramble

Created by Leslie, Scramble is a quick, kinesthetic way to practice the connections between vocabulary and related synonyms and antonyms. It's also an appropriate activity to use immediately after new words are introduced. Scramble is based on the idea of concept mapping, which is a strategy often used to show relationships among words. Many graphic organizers, such as Venn diagrams and semantic maps, develop word relationships through connecting concepts.

In Scramble, kids create a human concept map, arranging and rearranging groups representing word networks. Because Scramble is novel and physical, it helps students remember word connections. Because it requires students to practice appropriate behavior and collaboration, it increases social skills.

As mentioned in Chapter 4, our students wear lanyards with the vocabulary words (or synonyms or antonyms) they are responsible for explaining each day. We let them practice grouping with peers wearing related words; these students, in turn, become part of their entourage.

After we are sure that students know their word groups, we will randomly call out "Scramble!" throughout the day. Students with related synonyms and antonyms stand together in a huddle. We check to see if all the words are in the right entourage and help correct misconceptions before we send students back to their seats. After we have had kids Scramble a few times, we will have them switch cards so they have an opportunity to wear a different word. We then repeat the process.

One day Leslie summoned her fourth graders to Scramble. After checking that everyone was in the correct place, she said, "Take off your lanyard. Hold out your word. Now drop it!" Lanyards hit the floor. "Let's have a square dance!" she said.

Leslie clapped her hands and sang a hoedown song that she made up on the spot, "Swing around the room and dance, find a new word as fast as you can!" The kids skipped in a circle around the room. When she stopped singing, students picked up the closest lanyard and placed it around their necks.

"Great!" Leslie said, beaming, "Now you may go back to your seats. Get out your vocabulary journal and study your new word. How does your word connect with others?"

After giving them a few minutes to study their new words, Leslie called out, "Now eyeball who has the words that connect to yours. Give them the Old Vocabulary Stink Eye!" Then the human concept maps formed anew.

Leslie's intermediate students love to Scramble and often try to trick her into saying the word. As she walks around the room, she will sometimes hear a student nonchalantly ask in a quiet voice, "Hey, Ms. Montgomery, how do you like your eggs?"

This activity could easily become a free-for-all, but we don't let that happen. Visitors to our classrooms are usually impressed by the control the students demonstrate during Scramble. However, this is due to careful planning. Scramble must be practiced and modeled so that while students engage in this activity, they do not talk, run, or touch each other. We teach them to push their chairs in gently so no one will trip. Sometimes it takes modeling many times to make sure students understand how to participate appropriately.

Counting Dude, Bragging Dude

Research shows that students from low-income families often have experienced significantly fewer literacy interactions at home (Hart and Risley 1992). One of our goals is getting students to speak in complex sentences while practicing new vocabulary. Another goal is getting students to look each other in the eye, shake hands, and speak politely in social interactions. Counting Dude, Bragging Dude is an activity that helps them develop all those skills.

Our literacy coach shared the activity after attending a state professional development session conducted by consultant Jo Robinson. In our version, Counting Dudes line up on one side of the room and Bragging Dudes line up on the other. At a signal from the teacher, Counting Dudes and Bragging Dudes pair off, introduce themselves as their words, and begin the activity. Their objective: Bragging Dudes must create 7-Up sentences with the vocabulary words on their lanyards. Counting Dudes must determine the accuracy of their partner's choices.

If the Bragging Dude uses the word appropriately in a seven-word or longer sentence, he or she gets to give a quiet cheer, pat themselves on the back, dance a football jig, do a little hip-hop move, and so on. Then the Dudes exchange roles and the process is repeated. Each Dude then finds another partner in the class (see Figure 5.1).

Figure 5.1 *Allie states her sentence and DeEunique counts in Counting Dude, Bragging Dude.*

At the beginning of the year, we provide a scaffold for this activity by allowing students to write a 7-Up sentence on a card that they can carry with them. They may also keep their roles for several exchanges so they can practice the same sentence. As students participate in Counting Dude, Bragging Dude, they become more skilled at putting their words into longer sentences and they no longer need an anchor. They hear and speak more complex language, rather than only short declarative or imperative sentences or sentence fragments.

At first, they often create awkward sentences with grammatical errors. For example, second grader Leesa was quite proud of her sentence, "I was anxiously about walking to school by myself." Although we may wince when we hear such sentences, we know it is part of the academic risk-taking process and we have to give students some leeway initially. As students participate in Counting Dude, Bragging Dude throughout the school year, their sentences gradually become more sophisticated and accurate.

Let's listen to some conversations in Margot's classroom. Today, Dante wears a lanyard with the word *abundant*, which is one of the week's vocabulary words. Dante introduces himself to Jordan, who is wearing a card with *diversity*, a synonym for the vocabulary word *variety*, on his lanyard.

"Hello, my name is Abundant. I'm a vocabulary word," says Dante, holding out his hand for a handshake.

"Glad to meet you, Abundant. My name is Diversity, and I'm a synonym for Variety," replies Jordan, returning the shake.

Dante is the Bragging Dude, so he starts with his 7-Up sentence. "I bring in an abundant amount of income," he says slowly while Jordan, the Counting Dude, counts the words on his fingers.

"Eight!" exclaims Jordan. Dante does a fist pump to "brag" on his success.

Jordan takes his turn. "Our class has a diversity of kids."

Dante contemplates and proclaims the sentence is okay. It has seven words and uses the vocabulary word, although he adds, "I'm not really sure that sounds right."

Jordan does a little dance step, but looks thoughtful. Before he finds a new partner, he checks his vocabulary notebook again to think of another way he might use the word.

While students are engaged in this activity Margot circulates around the room and gently corrects any misconceptions. As a natural part of the mingling conversation, Margot may quietly do a quick reminder with Jordan and Dante on ways to use the word *diversity* in a sentence. After this, the boys will find new partners and try again.

Word Charades

Integrating drama and movement into vocabulary instruction has often been recommended, especially for English language learners (Alber and Foil 2003; Rieg and Paquette 2009). Because our students are also learning academic language, this is an especially appropriate activity for vocabulary practice in our classrooms. Creating a dramatic performance of the definition of a word is a way to help students internalize meanings and connect concepts. When our kids feel safe and comfortable in the classroom, they become expressive and enthusiastic about participating in activities that use drama and improvisation (see Figure 5.2).

In Word Charades (the "Wordless Silent Game"), students work in small groups and plan a charade to show the definition of the word. They dramatize the word silently while the rest of the students guess the word. A variation of Word Charades is Tableau, where a small group of students act out a word and then "freeze" in place so others can guess what the group is portraying (Wilhelm 1997). Show Me is like Word Charades, but is not necessarily silent. In Show Me, students draw a card with a word and then work in small groups to create dramatizations (usually a skit) that will

Figure 5.2 *Students act out the word* conviction.

enable their peers to guess the word. Dialogue and/or sound effects are permitted. Because we have worked hard to make sure our classrooms are places where kids feel free to take risks, Show Me has become one of their favorite activities.

The "talk" surrounding this activity also reinforces vocabulary learning. For example, Olivia, Charron, Shamyia, and Tayaunna stood in front of the class to act out their words.

The chart with the week's vocabulary words, their synonyms, and their antonyms rested on an easel at the side of the room. As the rest of the students watched intently, Charron silently moved to one side of the room and held up a handwritten paper that said, "Hot." Tayaunna walked to the other side of the room and held up a similar paper that said, "Cold." Meanwhile, Olivia stood at the cold side next to Tayaunna and wrapped her arms around her torso, pretending to shiver. Shamyia stood at the hot side and fanned herself as if she were sweating. Olivia and Shamyia then started flapping their arms like birds, and then each flew to the opposite side. Tayaunna and Charron walked to the middle and traded papers. Olivia and Shamyia flew back to the other side. The girls then met back in the middle, gave each other a group high five, and took a deep bow.

Leslie started the discussion, "What do you think their word is? Dante?"

Dante answered, "I think it's *migration*."

"Why do you think it was *migration*?" asked Leslie.

Dante replied, "Because Olivia was cold and she moved to a warm spot, and Shamyia was hot and she moved to a cold spot."

Leslie asked, "And why would a bird do that?"

Leslie waited a full ten seconds for Dante to answer, and then said, "Dante, I'll come back to you. Alexis, what do you think?

Alexis answered, "Well, I didn't think the word was *migration*. I thought the word was *adapt*."

Noah chimed in, "I thought that, too."

Leslie continued questioning. "Why did you think it was *adapt*, Alexis?"

Alexis replied, "Because they couldn't get used to a cold place so they moved to a warm place."

Leslie inserted a brief content lesson into the discussion. "I know in science we talked about how there are many forms of adaptation. You can stay where you are, you can move to another place, you can die . . . but let's think in terms of social studies right now as far as the word *adapt*. You're in an environment, you are in a region, that's your home. When you adapt to your environment you are not necessarily leaving it. Like on the Great Plains. What did the Native Americans do, Alexis?"

Alexis thought and then said, "They followed the food."

Leslie nodded. "They followed the food, but they stayed in the same region. They had seasons, so they transitioned from warm summers to harsh winters. How did they adapt to that? What do you think, Andrea?"

Andrea said, "They gathered up all their resources before times got tough so they would have them when they needed them."

"Right. They did a lot of hunting and growing the food they would need, and they stored it. Fabulous! Anybody else have an idea of what you think their word was? David?" asked Leslie.

David said, "I still think it is *migration*."

Leslie asked, "Why do you think it is *migration*?"

David began, "I think it's *migration* because . . ." He gave a complicated explanation describing each girl's every movement from a cool climate to a warm climate and back.

Leslie turned back to Dante. "Dante, why do you think birds would go from a cool climate to a warm climate? Why would birds go to a warmer place?"

"Well, now I think the word is *migration* because the birds are moving from a cold climate to a warm climate to be able to stay warm and find food," answered Dante.

Leslie smiled and said, "Good job, guys! Give them all a round of applause!"

One of our favorite charades occurred when Zahria handed Allie a pair of scissors and a piece of paper. Allie cut the piece of paper into half, and the two girls bowed. Dylan raised his hand and said, "I think the word is *segregate* because she is dividing one side from the other."

DeEunique disagreed. "No, I think it is *equality* because she divided them in equal halves."

Vocabulary Rap

As Duke Ellington said, "It don't mean a thing if it ain't got that swing," Many kids who cannot remember multiplication tables or spelling words can often remember and sing the lyrics to an entire catalog of songs. Music and rythmn are great motivators—exciting emotion, generating enjoyment, and boosting brain cells. Research has shown that music can help memory and retention (Wallace 1994) and is effective with learning disabled children (Gfeller 1986) and with students learning new languages (Brown and Perry 1991). When we insert music into our vocabulary lessons, we help students remember words.

Vocabulary Rap, described in Margot's classroom in the introduction, is one method we use to practice. Rap is a popular culture phenomenon that resonates with all types of students. There is some speculation that a hip-hop rhythm can help us remember (Borgia and Owles 2009/2010). The use of hip-hop and rap music to improve memory and retention can be found in content areas such as mathematics and some packaged vocabulary programs (for an example, see Flocabulary at www.flocabulary.com).

In our classrooms, we create an easy rap, including the vocabulary word, synonyms, and antonyms we are teaching. The structure is simple: "When I say _____ [vocabulary word], you say _____ [synonym]." After kids chant the vocabulary words and their synonyms, we repeat the with the antonyms. At the end of the rap, we call out "Freestyle!" and students do some inspired dance moves for a few seconds. As an extension, we sometimes ask kids to create their own simple hip-hop rhymes with their vocabulary words.

We find free, wordless hip-hop music on websites such as World HipHop Beats (www.worldhiphopbeats.com) or Creative Commons (www.creativecommons.org). We have found that instrumental hip-hop music with a rhythm of approximately eighty-four to ninety-four beats per minute is appropriate for Vocabulary Rap; that pace is fast enough to make it lively but not so fast that kids can't keep up. Once we download and store the music on the computer, we only have to push a button to play it at any time.

Vocabulary Rap is a quick, kinesthetic, whole-group activity. Students love moving their bodies to the hip-hop beat while they practice vocabulary connections and are often disappointed when it is time to stop.

Chain Link

One year Leslie's students were obsessed with the reading comprehension strategy of making connections, so much so that they would continue mentioning related ideas well beyond the literacy block. Leslie would try to get excited for them every time, but it didn't take long before the "connection craze" became a major distraction. To keep them focused, she asked the students to instead use a nonverbal cue, linking their fingers together like a chain whenever they made a connection to reading. This practice, reminiscent of Lori Ocskus's (2009) writing about interactive comprehension activities, proved so successful that Leslie decided to extend it to vocabulary instruction. The Chain Link game was born.

In Chain Link, students again create a human concept map (see Figure 5.3) to show extensions of meaning *beyond* synonyms and antonyms. Chain Link fosters creative and abstract thinking because students must delve deeper into the context of words.

Figure 5.3 *Chain Link, a vocabulary game in which students create a human concept map*

Students begin by wearing their vocabulary lanyards. We ask one student to go to the front of the room, pronounce his or her word, and state its meaning. The rest of the class contemplates ways their own words can connect to the first word. From volunteers, we choose a student to explain the link. If the link makes sense, the chosen student walks to the front of the room and links elbows with the first student. Now students must think of ways to connect with either the first or second student's word. Our students give intricate explanations as they continue to think of links, and they must continually revise their thinking as new words become the words to link. The kids just see it as a game where the object is to not be the last student sitting.

Chain Link is an activity that should be planned closer to the end of the vocabulary cycle, when students have had multiple exposures to the words and how they may be used. We model and practice so that students understand appropriate behavior and the creative thinking we expect. For this activity, we have found it is better to leave the vocabulary journals in the desks. We have observed that students rely too heavily on the "right" answer when they are permitted to consult their journals. Students are much more focused on how to apply words when they really have to think about the connections.

Chain Link also teaches students how to work with each other appropriately. As Leslie reminds the class in an amused voice, "This is a vocabulary activity. No one is getting married here. Remember that linking elbows is okay." Of course, the same goal could be accomplished with lengths of yarn or paper chains if you don't want your students to link elbows.

Leslie asks Melissa, who is wearing the word *port* on her lanyard, to stand at the front of the class. Dejaynae wears the words *reflection* and has already made a connection to *port* by stating that at a port, you can see the reflection of boats in the water.

Leslie continues, "Okay, now who has a connection to *port* or *reflection*? If you have a connection and I call on you, please begin by saying, 'My word is . . .' and then say the word and the connection. Tye?"

Tye states assertively, "My word is *harbor*, and I think I relate to *port* because a port means a safe place to load and unload cargo."

"Great!" exclaims Leslie. "Come on up here and join the chain!"

The activity continues with some students making immediate connections, some having to think hard to make a connection, and some making inaccurate connections. In every case, Leslie cheers them on or guides them to think of more appropriate word relationships. She reminds them that making these connections is like telling stories about the words in their heads. She provides wait time for students to think and insists that the connections make sense.

At the very end of the Chain Link, the challenge is to see who can link the two words at the end of the chain to complete the circle—a very creative task indeed!

Recently, Seth was at the end of the chain wearing the word *vast*. Jermaine was at the other end wearing the word *altitude*. After thinking a minute, Jermaine won the admiration of the entire class when he said, "I took a rocket ship to the satellite up in space and it was high up in altitude. The satellite gives us the Internet, which has a vast amount of information." The two boys linked elbows, and the chain was complete! Relating this story, Leslie mused, "There really are no losers in our game. We are a vocabulary community."

Small-Group and Independent Practice

Whole-group activities provide instruction and modeling, but small-group practice helps scaffold students toward independence. The right small-group combination can establish a low-risk environment where students can try out new learning in an enjoyable setting. Students usually enjoy working with their peers and often see small-group activities as a chance to have fun with their words. We have found that vocabulary instruction reinforces our classroom community to such a degree that we have to be less and less strategic about placement of students in small groups.

One caution: When students are first practicing application of new words, be diligent about monitoring small-group activities and listening to student discussions. Peer response often helps correct misconceptions and validates learning, but if misconceptions persist they are difficult to dislodge from students' memories. We want students to have an opportunity to share their work, not only for them to feel proud of their accomplishments but also so we can catch and correct misconceptions.

Vocabulary Board Games

Board games are always a popular and fun way for kids to practice vocabulary in small groups. We use teacher-created vocabulary board games to review and apply vocabulary definitions, synonyms, and antonyms. Like all teachers, we are always short on time to make materials, so we rely on free and inexpensive sources on the Internet to help us. EdHelper (www.edHelper.com) is a website filled with templates for a variety of activities. For a small subscription fee, we can download materials to make games and activities in several different subjects. To make our vocabulary board game, we click on the "Create Puzzles" section and find the "Vocabulary Board Game" link. There we can enter our own vocabulary words and print out the game board on paper. We laminate each game onto a manila folder and label it so we can easily store and reuse it later. We keep sets of game markers and dice in plastic bags for simple distribution and cleanup. These games can be used for review and future practice in literacy centers.

The board game we use follows a simple pathway, containing spaces for players to move. Vocabulary words appear in some of the spaces, and depending on how we have designed the board, the same words may appear twice in some games. The game is easy and quick to play: a student rolls the die and moves the designated number of spaces. If a student lands on a space with a vocabulary word, he performs one of several vocabulary activities depending on the guidelines we have set. We can ask students to use the word in a 7-Up sentence, discuss their synonyms and/or antonyms, or give the definition. Sometimes we ask students to decide on their own style for the game. Once, a small group of third-grade students chose to only allow sentences with exclamation points!

The other students in the group decide whether the answer is correct. We have found that if the group members cannot agree, they will usually find a way to check the answer (using vocabulary journals, anchor charts, or other resources in the room) or will call us over to settle the question. If the answer is correct, the player may roll again. If the player is incorrect, he or she stays on the space and tries again next time. The group reserves the right to ask the first person to land on "Finish" to use any word on the board in a sentence. If the sentence is correct, the winner is declared. If the answer is incorrect, that person must go all the way back to "Start" and begin again.

Although the goal of such games is giving students fun ways to practice applying vocabulary, the conversations about words often deepen their understanding of concept development as well. In Margot's third-grade classroom, for example, Taylor, Jaden, Korey, and Diamond are focused on six science-related terms: *crater, speck, perceive, telescope, asteroid,* and *satellite.* This group has decided the activity will be "individual's choice" when they land on a word. Students have several options when they land on a word. They can use the word in a 7-Up sentence, create a sentence using a synonym or antonym (as long as the student designates this option and the sentence makes sense), or use the definition in context.

Margot circulates to monitor the children's responses. "While you are playing your board game today, remember we are working on articulation. I want you to articulate your words and sentences when you speak," she reminds them.

Jaden rolls the die, counts five spaces, and lands on the word *telescope.* He thinks a minute and then says, "When I was using my telescope I saw a half moon." Taylor, Korey, and Diamond nod their heads in approval. Jaden has created an accurate sentence that has more than seven words and has articulated well. He gets to roll again and lands on a blank space.

Diamond takes her turn. She rolls the die and lands on the word *satellite.* She contemplates out loud, "There are two meanings to *satellite.* I'm not sure which one to use. Like, there's the moon satellites the earth and there is a satellite that gets us Internet and stuff. Hmm." She mulls it over, and then says, "Okay, my sentence is 'I couldn't get the Internet because the satellite wasn't working.'" The other students in the group are good with that sentence, and Korey gives her a high five. She rolls again.

Diamond shows us the power of teaching kids to think aloud. We should also note that we work on multiple meanings when we introduce the words and when we add synonyms and antonyms, but we have usually chosen a meaning for emphasis during the vocabulary cycle. In this case, we had specified *satellite* would be used in its noun form—as a thing. Diamond used knowledge from a classroom discussion about multiple meanings when she waivered in using the word *satellite* as a noun or verb in her sentence.

It's Taylor's turn next. She lands on the word *perceive*. After a brief pause, she says, "I perceive a rock on the ground." Her sentence has exactly seven words, but as Jaden points out, "That doesn't make that much sense." Although Taylor explains that she meant the definition of perceive as "see," the group decides that she needs to try again. She accepts her peers' decision with grace and begins contemplating a more appropriate sentence that she might say the next time.

Korey's roll lands him on another space with the word *telescope*. "I think I'll use the antonym." He sits in thought for a few seconds. "I use a microscope to see things closer." He looks around the group, beaming.

"Actually, it's not really the antonym of *telescope* the way you used it," says Jaden.

Margot has been circulating and hones in on this discussion. "Jaden's right. You have to be more specific," she says to Korey, and he starts thinking anew.

The game continues until Taylor lands on the last space. Her challenge, decided by her group members, is to use the word *telescope* again in a unique way. She is declared the winner with the sentence, "I used a telescope to diminish large objects into small objects."

Vocabulary Rings

More than two thousand years ago, Aristotle said, "Exercise in repeatedly recalling a thing strengthens the memory." Research suggests that testing memory, sometimes called *retrieval practice*, can actually aid in learning (Roediger and Butler 2011; Roediger and Karpicke 2006). In cognitive science, this phenomenon is called the *testing effect*. Retrieval practice is the idea behind activities such as using flash cards to practice word recollection. Vocabulary Rings are a new twist. We don't use them to drill vocabulary. Rather, we use them to make retrieval practice a collaborative and fun activity that continues to help build word schema.

To make Vocabulary Rings, we give each student index cards and labels representing the vocabulary words we have taught for this cycle. The students peel off each label and stick it to the top center of one side of each card. After students know the expectations, we give them blank cards and let them write their words themselves, but at the beginning we want to make sure the words are spelled correctly.

Underneath the word label, students draw a simple picture to serve as a logographic cue (Beers 2003) to help them remember the definition. On the other side of the card, students write a seven-word sentence that includes the word. Next, they attach the finished cards to a binder ring, so they can carry the vocabulary words with them like a set of keys. Each time students make new cards, they add them to their ring.

Students often test themselves or a classmate, pairing up to use their Vocabulary Rings (see Figure 5.4). Students also can group and regroup their cards by themes as a sorting activity. Because we often see kids checking their Vocabulary Rings as a quick reference during other activities, we consider Vocabulary Rings another resource in the class.

Another way to use Vocabulary Rings is in a game we call Line It Up, which can be played in a whole group or in a teacher-directed small group (see Figure 5.5). To play this game, we ask students to line up the vocabulary cards by clues. For example, we will say, "In the first position, put the card that means _____." Students find the card on their Vocabulary Ring, open the ring, and take off the word (often we will have them take off the words they will be using for the game ahead of time). They place the word card at the top of their desks. Then we will call on a student to give the clue for the word that will go in the second position, underneath the first word. The student must decide on a word and give a definition as a clue for the rest of the class. We always play the game using the words from the current vocabulary cycle, but sometimes we make it more challenging toward the end by adding a few words they have learned before.

Figure 5.4 *Dasia and Diamond practice with Vocabulary Rings.*

Figure 5.5 *A student uses Vocabulary Ring cards to play Line It Up.*

After all the word cards are in place, we ask students to flip the cards over to see if they have the right words in the correct position. We always have to remember to jot down the words and the definitions students gave on a scrap of paper. If one of our kids loses his or her place or drops a card, we don't want to waste precious time trying to reconstruct the entire game.

Word Colors

Historical research suggests that socioeconomic status and conceptual thinking are related, with children from low-income families showing more literal thinking than students who have had more economic advantages (Siller 1957). This makes sense when we remember the research about socioeconomic background and vocabulary development that showed higher-income preschoolers knew almost four times as many words in their vocabulary banks as their lower-income counterparts when they began school (Hart and Risley 1995). For vocabulary instruction to be meaningful for our students, it has to go beyond memory practice.

Word Colors is an activity that was shared by one of our Atkinson colleagues. We ask students to write a sentence or paragraph recalling a personal experience or content connection with a word, and then we ask them to choose a color that might represent the word. In Word Colors, our kids have a chance to practice higher-level thinking as they review definitions of the words (see Figure 5.6).

Each student receives an index card with a vocabulary word written in marker. On one side of the card, the student uses a crayon or colored pencil to shade the background of the card in their chosen color. On the other side, they write an explanation of the color they chose to symbolize the word. We ask them to use only one color; otherwise they have a tendency to draw a picture. We have found that struggling learners often go straight to something they already know. We want them to use a color to represent the meaning of the word using higher-order thinking.

We are constantly delighted by the creative thinking our students demonstrate when they are encouraged to do so. For example, we recently taught words from a social studies unit and used Word Colors to practice. Some examples of Word Color representations our students made included:

Figure 5.6 *Justice reviews her Word Color cards.*

Red is for segregate because bricks are red and they can separate people.
Green is for freedom because if you have freedom you can run in the grass.

The word *swift* had varied interpretations:

I think black for swift because I think of a Ninja.
Swift is yellow because when you move super fast you feel like a ball of fire.
I choose brown for swift because when you are being swift
    on the ground you can pick up dirt.
I used brown for swift because it is the color of me and I am swift.

Word Colors is an easy independent activity, but the thinking behind it is much more complex. By linking colors to their words, students are creating visual representations in their minds and making connections to meaning that can help them recall the words later.

A variation of Word Colors is to use paint swatches from a hardware store and ask students to choose the shade that would match their word and then explain why. Although we first heard about the use of color cards to represent a reader's level of understanding in Tammy McGregor's *Comprehension Connections* (2007), we have found that students can also use these tools to deepen their understanding of vocabulary.

Word Illustrations

As mentioned previously, we encourage the use of logographic cues by having students draw a picture to represent a word in their vocabulary journals and elsewhere to help them remember the meaning. Word Illustrations enable students to further demonstrate their understanding of vocabulary words through visual representations.

In this activity, students illustrate vocabulary words by combining the word and the meaning into a drawing. We give students a graphic organizer of a chart with each vocabulary word in a separate box. We then challenge them to find creative ways to incorporate the words within a picture. For example, if the word *pollinate* has been introduced, a student may choose to draw two flowers and show how an insect is carrying the letters of the word *pollinate* from one flower to another (see Figure 5.7).

When they are first learning this technique, students will often draw just a picture and not incorporate the word, or they might write the word above a simple drawing of the word. To encourage more complex imagery, we show them how to do word illustrations as a whole group and then ask those who seem to understand the concept to display their work on a document camera so they can explain their thinking for the rest of the

Figure 5.7 *A student's word illustrations*

class. After seeing several examples, struggling students tend to have a better understanding of what we expect and will usually try to revise their word illustrations to express more conceptual thinking.

Fifth-grader Maddy demonstrated a great example of the word *era* by making the *e* into a picture of a woman wearing a long dress and a pompadour hairstyle, the *r* into a woman wearing a shorter dress and high heels, and the *a* into a girl wearing her hair in a ponytail, with jeans and a T-shirt. Maddy's explanation? Pointing to the first letter, she said, "I made this because . . . you know how in the 1600s the women wore different clothes like big poofy dresses? This one has a big wig and flowers in her hair." Pointing to the *r* she explained, "This one is from later." As she pointed to the *a*, she said, "This is now. We can dress any way we want and we can have any hairstyle we want." At prompting from her teacher, she added, "This shows how clothes and hairstyles have changed in different eras."

Peter shared his word illustration of the word *explorer*. He had used crayons to draw a picture of a yellow sun, green trees in the background, and a brown hill with a black entrance way into a cave. He depicted the word *explorer* by making each letter a different color and giving it a pair of feet.

nomadic

Figure 5.8 *David's drawing of the vocabulary word* nomadic

David explained his drawing of *nomadic* (see Figure 5.8). The *n* was the face of a Native American boy, the *o* was a basket, and the *m* was an oversized mountain with arrows showing the way over. The rest of the letters were part of a village, with the *a* as a buffalo, the *d* as a tipi, the *i* as a tree, and the *c* as a person. "The early Native Americans were nomadic. They had to go over mountains to find food," he said, clarifying.

PowerPoint Portrayals

Using multimedia to develop ideas is a component of the Common Core State Standards (Anchor Standard 5 for Speaking and Listening). According to Rebecca Mullen and Linda Wedwick (2008), "Being literate no longer only involves being able to read and write. The literate of the twenty-first century must be able to download, upload, rip, burn, chat, save, blog, Skype, IM, and share" (66). By including technology in our vocabulary instruction, we can help prepare students for the future. College and career-ready students must also be able to give an oral presentation. Reporting on a topic with descriptive details while speaking clearly at an understandable pace is included in the Common Core State Standards (Anchor Standard 4 for Speaking and Listening).

One of the ways we integrate technology and oral presentations as part of vocabulary study is to have our students create PowerPoint Portrayals of a word (Dalton and Grisham 2011). We recognize that we are in the very early stages of technology integration and that PowerPoint is not the most advanced application available today. The same activity could be accomplished using other digital tools, such as Google Presentations, Animoto, Photo Story, or VoiceThread. The point of the assignment is to be purposeful about the text, colors, objects, and sound effects students choose to demonstrate their understanding of vocabulary. When they present the word in class, we ask them to follow an outline in which they introduce themselves with a title slide, explain each slide, ask if there are any questions, answer the questions, and thank the audience. The audience's job is to listen carefully, ask good questions, make the speaker feel appreciated, and complete a peer evaluation form (see Appendix F for a blank Peer- and Self-Evaluation Form).

When our students first do this activity, they have problems with organization and coherence, but they have no problem with enthusiasm for the technology and their topic. With more practice, they concentrate on enhancing the PowerPoint content and make deeper connections to the word.

When Leslie called on Alexis to present, for example, she clicked on her first slide, which contained a bright green background with her name in white letters. Alexis next clicked her second and only other slide, which showed a crumpled black and white photograph of a man in a military uniform. On the right was a photograph of an index card where Alexis had written, "Contribution story. My grandpa was always a good influence/contribution to me. He used to take me to his work and say, 'I hope you go to college and get you a good job.'" Underneath the photograph, she had pasted the word *contribution* in dark green 3-D letters.

Reading her index card, one might wonder if Alexis really understood the appropriate use of the word *contribution*. Her oral presentation revealed more knowledge. In a loud, clear voice she said, "This word is important to me because my grandpa was important to me. My grandpa made a contribution to the United States. He served our country in the war. And I also chose the color green because my grandpa's favorite color was green." Sweeping her arm like Vanna White, she read the index card aloud with expression and enthusiasm. Then she turned back to face the audience and asked, "Any questions?"

Vanessa raised her hand. "What war was he in?"

"World War II," Alexis replied confidently. "He was really my great-grandpa. Any other questions? Catlyn?"

"Where was he when he faced the enemy?" asked Catlyn. Alexis looked at Leslie, as if asking her for help.

Leslie came to her rescue: "We haven't really studied World War II yet, have we, Alexis?"

David piped up from the back of the room, saying, "I can clarify." David is a military buff and reads constantly about World War II. "He probably fought against the Rising Sun, which was Japan. It really depends on where he was. Was he in the Pacific or in Europe?"

"I don't really know that much about the war. I just know he was in it," answered Alexis, with a little squirm.

"Well, that would be a good question to ask your family," said Leslie.

Alexis looked relieved and smiled at her audience, before saying, "Thanks for watching!" The students clapped and Alexis walked back to her seat. She took a minute to fill out a self-evaluation form about her presentation and then handed it to a classmate to fill out a peer evaluation. Completing peer- and self-evaluations help students solidify what is expected the next time they do a presentation.

In addition to helping students develop speaking skills and apply technology, Power-Point Portrayals give students authentic and meaningful connections to vocabulary words. This was clear in Stacie's talk. After moving through her introductory slide, which included her name, she deftly touched her finger to the electronic whiteboard to move her PowerPoint to the next slide. There was a booming sound effect as the slide showed a photograph of a package of birthday candles on the left side of the screen and a package of batteries on the right side. "I chose this picture to represent *scarcity* because when we had the flood last year there was a scarcity of things. I chose the word *scarcity* because it happened to me before and I really know this word well." She tapped the screen and the word *scarcity* appeared.

Next she pulled up a slide with a photograph of Angela Johnson's picture book *The Sweet Smell of Roses*. "I also chose the word *depend* because it's meaningful to me and I depend on a lot of people. I chose this picture book to represent the word *depend* because this book has a cover on it and the book depends on the cover to keep it from getting damaged."

In discussing their presentations, Leslie said, "You all could pick the words you wanted from this vocabulary cycle. A lot of you picked *scarcity* and I know that many of us have had a time in our lives where we have felt a scarcity of something. It seems to be a pretty meaningful word to a lot of you. Was there a reason that *scarcity* stood out for you?"

Maria answered, "Because my mom didn't have a job and we had a scarcity of food." Many of the students in this class nodded in empathy.

Connected Words Are Remembered Words

There are a variety of ways to practice vocabulary. Looking up definitions, completing worksheets, and sitting through flash-card drills are traditional methods, but in our experience they never got kids excited about learning new words and were not very effective in helping them learn. We want our students to look forward to vocabulary practice. With activities that incorporate art, movement, technology, music, drama, public speaking, and more, vocabulary practice can not only motivate students to learn but also ensure that they remember more.

Chapter 6

Celebrate to Validate

Celebrate! Celebrate! Dance to the music!
—Three Dog Night

In her beautiful picture book *I'm in Charge of Celebrations* (1995), Byrd Baylor writes, "You can tell what's worth a celebration because your heart will POUND and you'll feel like you're standing on top of a mountain and you'll catch your breath like you were breathing some new kind of air."

The ability to use new vocabulary with confidence is similarly exhilarating, empowering, and expansive. When high-risk students learn words that increase their vocabulary knowledge, we need to celebrate their progress. Before our summative vocabulary assessments, we always honor learning. Our celebrations come near the end of a vocabulary cycle and, at first glance, can look like vocabulary practice. However, there is a subtle but important difference. In vocabulary practice, students are taking tentative steps. They are trying out words and often make mistakes. In vocabulary celebration, students have become more comfortable using new words and confidently engage in activities to review and apply the terms in context.

We love parties, and so do our kids. We use music, food, games, and anything else that we can think of to give our vocabulary celebrations a party atmosphere. At a Vocabulary Party, we find ways to rejoice in words. We help students review new vocabulary and recognize hard work and learning. We also use these sessions to teach the art of social talk and reinforce team spirit.

Block Party

Betty Hart and Todd Risley (1992), the researchers who found that children from low-income families learn fewer words before starting school, also note that they typically engage in less open-ended conversation than students who come from more privileged backgrounds. A Block Party helps close the gap. We enable students to apply vocabulary while learning how to converse in a social setting.

Block Party is based on the concept of neighborhood gatherings. Just as neighbors might have a barbecue or festival to learn more about each other, participants at a vocabulary Block Party use their words to meet, greet, and mingle. This promotes a sense of community and helps students develop social skills as they discuss the meanings of their words.

Welcome, Words!

In Margot's third-grade class, students are wearing word lanyards. A silver tray of sugar cookies sits on a small table near the front beside a small stack of festive paper napkins. Margot explains the Block Party to her students. "When I call out a vocabulary word, that person needs to stand up and invite his synonyms and antonyms to his party. Make sure there are no party crashers! After that, I am going to ask you to mingle and meet people who are not related to your word."

Margot calls Barlyn and Emily up to the front of the classroom to remind students how to be good Block Party participants. The students have practiced this activity many times before, but every so often Margot models appropriate behavior again to make sure they remember how to do it well. "When you meet each other, introduce yourselves and shake hands. Say something like, 'Hi! My name is _____ and I am an antonym for _____.'" Barlyn and Emily try it out for the rest of the class.

"Nice job, girls," Margot says afterward. "Now tell a little bit about yourselves. Remember, you are pretending to be the word you are wearing. You can chat about your definition, tell a sentence you might be in, or just talk about ways you might be used. Let the other person really get to know you."

Barlyn and Emily nod that they understand and take their seats.

"Okay, let's get started," says Margot. "I'd like to welcome you to our vocabulary Block Party today! The first word I would like to invite to our party is the word that means 'a possible selection.'"

Sylvia stands up.

Margot continues, "Okay, let's start with you, Miss Alternative. Who would you like to invite to the party?"

"Well, first, I'd like to invite my synonyms to my party," Sylvia says. Jaydin, with the word *choice* and Kevan, wearing the word *substitute*, stand up and join Sylvia at the front of the room. Sylvia says, "Welcome, words!" and then invites her antonyms. *Same* and *usual* join the party. Margot calls the rest of the vocabulary terms by stating their definitions, and one by one, each "word" invites the related synonyms and antonyms to a conversation.

Once all the words are assembled with their entourages, the party starts. Margot pushes a button on her computer and soft music fills the classroom. Students begin to mingle, meeting and greeting each other and introducing themselves as their words (see Figure 6.1). At a Block Party, words do not have to be related to converse with each other.

Margot announces, "Now, everyone mingle!"

"Hi, my name is Alternative, and I mean a different choice. What's your name?" Sylvia says to Micah, who is wearing the word *structure*.

Micah replies, "My name is Structure. My definition is something that is built. What are some examples of an alternative?"

Sylvia thinks, then responds, "Well, if I pick a hamburger instead of chicken nuggets for lunch, that's an alternative. What are examples of structures?"

Figure 6.1 *Dajianna and T.J. discuss their vocabulary words at a Block Party.*

"My examples would be a bridge or a building. That's a structure," answers Micah. "What is your favorite antonym?"

"My favorite antonym is *usual*, like 'I'll just have the usual,'" Sylvia replies. "What's yours?"

Sylvia and Micah continue to ask each other questions and chat about their words, their definitions, examples, and their application in sentences. Then they say good-bye and move on to a different partner. There is no set conversation guideline to follow except that they must role-play their words. Through academic discussion and plenty of practice, students have learned to talk about these words and are on their way to elaborated answers.

As students socialize while role-playing their words, Margot gives each child a napkin and serves a cookie from the tray. Students acknowledge the treat with a "thank you" and politely eat their cookies as they continue conversing with their partners. While students chat about their words, Margot listens, informally assessing student knowledge. By this time, students have had many experiences with the words during the vocabulary cycle, so few of them have difficulties using the words in context. For students who still might be confused, Margot gently encourages them to check the available resources, such as vocabulary journals, anchor charts, Vocabulary Rings, or the sentence stems on back of the cards they are wearing. Margot also corrects misconceptions if she hears a student use a word inaccurately. Now *is* the time to make sure that students are precise in word use.

An unmistakable sense of confidence permeates the classroom as students who did not know many of these words a few days ago now use them with ease. Margot brings the party to a close. "Night is coming," she announces. "It's time to tell your word friends good-bye and go home to bed. Lights off!" She switches off the overhead lights in the classroom. The students scamper to their seats and lay their heads on their desks. Soft exaggerated snoring sounds can be heard (as well as a few giggles, of course) as students pretend to sleep.

Margot lets the room become calm, and then snaps the light back on. "Good morning, children! Who can tell me something they learned at the Block Party?" Margot asks a few students to debrief their vocabulary learning by recounting some of their conversations. This is one more time for students to hear words appropriately in context.

When Margot decides students are ready, she makes her last announcement. "It is now time to eat breakfast and have our assessment." She gives each student a napkin with a few pieces of toasted oat cereal. Students snack on their "breakfast" while completing their vocabulary assessment.

Toasting Party

The students in Leslie's intermediate class are partial to a celebration they call the Toasting Party or "Hear, hear!" Students offer their favorite words and the rest of the class offers a toast in celebration. Students then mingle and chat about their words in a social setting.

The Toasting Party gives students a chance to demonstrate their knowledge. It doesn't matter what vocabulary word they choose as long as they give an academic explanation. Because peers join in the celebration, students feel validated.

Celebrating Velcro Words

In Leslie's fourth-grade classroom, Davion passes out the lanyards. The words for the week are *dense*, *surround*, *region*, *solution*, and *canyon*. An anchor chart on the wall displays two synonyms (examples) and two antonyms (non-examples) for each vocabulary word, making twenty-five words in all.

Davion speaks up first. "Ms. Montgomery, we have more words than we do people today!"

"No problem," says Leslie. She turns to the class. "Do I have a couple of volunteers who will challenge themselves with extra words?" At least six hands shoot into the air.

While words are being assigned, Leslie asks some students to help her pour juice into small plastic cups, which she then serves.

"Remember, we want to celebrate Velcro words—those words that will stick to your brain!" Leslie says.

Charron raises her hand. "I'll start." After getting the nod from Leslie, Charron says, "I like the word *solution*. I think it's a Velcro word because it's a much better word than just 'answer.' It makes you sound smarter."

Leslie asks, "When can you use the word *solution*?"

"Well," answers Charron, "you can have the solution to a problem in real life or the solution to a math problem."

Leslie looks around at the class and sees that most of the students are nodding their heads in agreement. "Charron, we appreciate the word *solution* and celebrate its use. Hear, hear!"

The students raise their glasses and intone, "Hear, hear!" Then they each take a sip of juice.

Daniel speaks next. "I'll go. I think the words *sparse* and *scanty* are Velcro words because I never heard them before. Now I know they are good antonyms for the word *dense*."

Leslie says, "*Sparse* and *scanty*. Hear, hear!"

"Hear, hear!" repeat the students, and then sip from their cups.

"Madison, would you like to share your word?" Leslie asks a girl with blue glasses perched on her freckled nose.

"Well, my favorite word is the word *hypothesis* because it's an antonym for *solution* and it is a good word in science that means *guess*. We can use it when we are making predictions," says Madison earnestly.

"We celebrate the word *hypothesis*. Hear, hear!" Leslie raises her cup in celebration, and the students follow suit.

Leslie next calls on Dejaynae. "Dejaynae, what word would you like to celebrate?"

Dejaynae is ready with an answer. "My favorite word is *region* because *region* means a country or a state that can be separated into different parts."

"We like your word! *Region*! Let's celebrate your word! Hear, hear!" Leslie says.

Students continue to announce their favorite words, and their classmates continue to celebrate their choices. Leslie says, "Now let's mingle! Remember, we want to use our best manners and make a good impression on the other people at the party."

Students find partners and begin to chat with each other about the words on their lanyards. They also engage in open-ended conversation about vocabulary, much like they do in the Block Party. They group and regroup as they sip their juice and discuss definitions, sentences, ways to use the words, and why they think their word is or is not a Velcro word. If anyone spills the juice, that student cleans it up but, surprisingly, we have had very few accidents. We think it is because this is truly a social event, like a college reception, where they are expected to use their manners and put their best foot forward.

When Leslie calls the Toasting Party to a close, students are ready to take their summative assessment for this vocabulary cycle. They are relaxed and confident in their ability to demonstrate their knowledge.

Jeopardy! Party

Kids love playing games. Because our students feel part of a vocabulary team, they participate in game parties enthusiastically and appropriately. *Jeopardy!* has been part of American television for years. In this game, contestants are given the answers and must come up with the questions. A quick Internet search will yield several websites with *Jeopardy!* templates and music. Some of the sites have host Alex Trebeck announcing, "THIS IS *JEOPARDY!*" When the *Jeopardy!* jingle begins to play in the classroom, our students get ready for some vocabulary game action to celebrate their learning.

As often as possible, we try to involve students in writing the questions for games. Students get four index cards apiece and write two questions featuring the current vocabulary words, synonyms, or antonyms, and two questions for words they have learned in the past. Without guidance, students usually write questions such as "How do you spell . . . ?" Before we play *Jeopardy!* the first time, we model how to write different types of questions, which can be fill-in-the-blank or cloze sentences, matching word and definition, or What Am I?– type questions. We encourage students to "dazzle" us with their questions, but the point is that students take ownership. If they can write the questions, then they know the answers. Plus, they feel like rock stars when their question comes up!

To play *Jeopardy!* in the classroom, we bring out an *Eggspert* game system (Educational Insights) that can either be used with an AC adapter or with batteries. A wireless version is also available. The *Eggspert* consists of six colored egg-shaped answer buzzers and a control button. For our version of *Jeopardy!* we divide our classes into teams, each paired with a different-colored buzzer. We read the student-generated answer card aloud, set the timer, and listen for the game-show ticking to begin. The student who is representing each team buzzes to answer, and the colored egg of the quickest contestant lights up. The buzzer dings, and the student answers in the form of a question. Because of the nature of this game, the question usually follows the "What is _____?" pattern. A word under study fits in the blank.

"This Is Gonna Be Fun!"

Margot announces, "Today we are going to have a *Jeopardy!* Party!"

As the *Jeopardy!* theme music fills the air, students exclaim, "This is gonna be fun!" and "We played this game last time! *Jeopardy!* is *so* fun!"

Margot turns off the music and begins dividing the students into teams. "If your word means 'a small stream,' please stand up." A girl with braids wearing the word *creek* stands up.

Margot continues, "Thank you, Cindy. Synonyms and antonyms of *creek*, please join Cindy.

"Team Creek, you have the purple buzzer. Please come up to these four seats." She continues with Team Voyage (green), Team Coast (yellow), Team Distinguish (pink), and Team Popular (blue).

Margot starts the game. She announces, "Welcome to Vocabulary *Jeopardy!*" She hums the *Jeopardy!* theme and the students join in (see Figure 6.2).

As the melody ends, Margot says, "Remember, the answer has to be in the form of a question." She then picks up a stack of cards with answers and questions the students wrote the day before.

"Okay, here's the first one. 'A synonym of *coast* is _____.'"

The blue egg buzzes. Michael, the first player on Team Popular, says, "What is *shore*?"

"Right!" says Margot. The blue team cheers. Margot then has all the students in the class repeat the correct answer in a self-assured voice. She wants them to internalize a correct answer and continue to build word confidence.

Play continues until the time is up. Margot asks the last question. Teams

Figure 6.2 *Margot facilitates* Jeopardy.

confer, coming up with an answer and a wager. The captain of each team writes the wager and the question on a marker board. A winner is declared and the winning team takes a bow.

Deal or No Deal Party

When we announce a *Deal or No Deal* Party, the room buzzes with excitement. *Deal or No Deal* is a popular television game show where a contestant chooses one suitcase out of a set of twenty-six, each with a different sum of money, from $.01 to $1,000,000. At each turn, the contestant tries to guess which suitcases contain amounts lower than the one chosen and eliminate them from the board. Along the way, a "banker" calls the contestant on the telephone and offers a deal—does the contestant want to keep the money the banker is offering or take a chance that the chosen suitcase contains more cash? The contestant has to decide whether to take the deal or keep guessing. On the TV show, the contestant gets to keep the cash. In the classroom, our kids play so earnestly you would think they were going to leave with a wheelbarrow full of money, like Scrooge McDuck!

We use free online templates to play *Deal or No Deal* (these can be found on several different websites). We project the *Deal or No Deal* website onto the electronic whiteboard, with the theme music, colors, and sound effects from the show. To prepare for the game, students again write their own questions on index cards about the vocabulary words, the synonyms, and the antonyms. At first, we facilitate the game, but often as the year progresses and students get better at speaking in front of the group, we ask a student emcee to read the questions.

We like *Deal or No Deal* because each student plays individually by writing his or her answers on small dry erase boards, holding the boards in the air (see Figure 6.3). Immediately, we can do an informal assessment of all our students by glancing at the answers around the room. We can also tell how long it takes for students to remember the words. When all the whiteboards are held up in the air, we call on one of the students. The student answers the question and gets to choose a suitcase to be eliminated for the class.

When the banker calls, students write "Deal" or "No Deal" on the dry erase boards. The majority wins, and the class decides either to take the banker's deal or to keep on guessing. It is amazing how seriously the students take this decision, debating the merits and probability of the money that may be left on the board.

After questions have been read, we keep them for the next time. During a bonus round we ask students to recall previously learned words and their synonyms and antonyms.

Figure 6.3 *Dajianna shows answers in* Deal or No Deal.

Big Winners

On a Friday morning, Leslie says, "Let's have a *Deal or No Deal* Party!" An audible buzz fills the classroom as the kids anticipate playing the game.

"Don't forget! You may use your vocabulary journals to help you. In fact, you may use any resources that are in the room. And remember, I'm not looking for who can write the answer the fastest—I'm looking for the correct answer."

Leslie reads the first student-created sentence, "Give me a sentence with the word *invertebrate*." Each student diligently writes a sentence on his or her whiteboard with the marker and holds the whiteboard in the air.

Leslie calls on Katlin to read her sentence: "A worm in the ground is a invertebrate." After a brief class discussion about the accurate use of the articles *a* and *an*, Leslie tells Katlin to choose a suitcase. Katlin selects suitcase number eight, which opens to reveal $50. The class squeals with delight. The big prize of $1,000,000 is still on the board somewhere!

After several more questions, such as "What is an antonym of the word *characteristic*?" and "What does it mean to *flourish*?" a phone rings. Words appear on the screen to inform students that the banker is calling. The banker offers them $11,000 to end the game. "No deal! No deal!" the students call excitedly, shaking their heads and pointing their thumbs to the ground.

"Are you sure?" asks Leslie. "You can buy a lot of things with $11,000. A car, put a down payment on a house. . . ."

The students are firm. "No! Still no deal!" they shout with determination.

Leslie calls their attention to the fraction of possibilities left. "You know, you can figure out what the possibilities are to get to the $1,000,000." She demonstrates a simple probability lesson. By the end of the game, students are not only writing the answers to the questions, they are also writing fractions to represent the opportunities left to get to $1,000,000.

It is getting close to the end of the game. The question is "What is a synonym of *ambition*?" Stevin pipes up. "That was my question! I used a word from last year!"

After they answer the question on their whiteboards, Daniel is asked to answer the question and choose a suitcase. He picks suitcase number five, but the banker calls and offers $128,000. The class calls with enthusiasm, "Deal! Deal!" Leslie, with a nod, taps "yes" on "Take the deal," and then taps on suitcase number twelve, the one they had chosen at the beginning of the game. It opens to reveal $750. The room erupts in animated cheers. They are big winners!

Charades or Show Me Party

Although we use Charades or Show Me as a practice activity, the students love it so much we often reinstitute it as a vocabulary celebration. The announcement of a Charades or Show Me Party always gets a cheer. We divide the class into small groups. Each small group randomly gets one of the vocabulary words. Each team has ten minutes to create a charade or skit that demonstrates its word (see Figure 6.4). In Charades, students must create a skit that is silent. In Show Me, talking and sound effects are allowed. Because the students have had so much practice with the words, they are comfortable creating and participating in skits for their peers to guess.

Once the time is up, all the groups come back together. Each member of the audience gets a marker and a small dry erase board and the performances begin. As each group is performing, the audience members write down their word guesses. This is a quick way to hold all students accountable, assess their knowledge, and keep them engaged. Because today is a

Figure 6.4 *Jaheim, VeAsia, and Diamond dramatize the word passage at a Charades Party.*

celebration and not a game, there are no winners or losers.

After all the groups have performed, as a review we discuss what they have learned over the course of this vocabulary cycle. Students turn and talk to a partner and reflect on how their knowledge of the words has increased. This reflection time also gives students a chance to correct each other's misconceptions.

Other Party Ideas

Over the years, we have hosted many different Vocabulary Parties. The students came up with several of these ideas.

- Dance Party—Students answer a vocabulary question and do some moves to dance music.
- Luau Party (see Figure 6.5)—Students answer a vocabulary question while doing the limbo to reggae music. Serve Hawaiian Punch.
- American Idol Party—Students use a plastic microphone and sing a few lines of a song they have created about their vocabulary word.
- Art Show Party—Students mingle and discuss artwork they have created depicting vocabulary words.
- Holiday Parties—Students enjoy a special holiday treat while discussing their vocabulary words. Here are some suggested thematic questions:
  - Fall Festival—Why is your word a treat?
  - Thanksgiving—Why are you thankful for your word?
  - Winter Holiday—Why is your word a gift?
  - Valentine's Day—Why do you love your word?
  - St. Patrick's Day—Why will your word bring you luck?

The Power of Celebration

We believe vocabulary learning is worth honoring with activities that are fun and engaging, helping our students gain confidence and command of words. A vocabulary celebration acts as a review before a summative assessment and a validation of student learning. As students par-

ticipate in a Vocabulary Party, they have opportunities to apply vocabulary to new situations, correct misconceptions, participate in social events, and expand their network of words.

Figure 6.5 *Phillip enjoys doing the limbo at a Vocabulary Luau.*

Author Thomas Peters, a business leader and speaker, has said, "Celebrate what you want to see more of." In our classrooms, we want to see more of our students using new vocabulary confidently, but we also want them to feel joyful about their growing facility with words. Vocabulary Parties let us tap into the playful spirit of elementary students while honoring their increasingly sophisticated word knowledge.

Chapter 7

Spreading Vocabulary Wings

Sometimes words are not enough.
—Lemony Snicket

In the book *Miss Alaineus: A Vocabulary Disaster* (Frasier 2000), fifth grader Sage is absent from school on Vocabulary Day in her classroom. Her friend, Starr, calls with the words Sage is supposed to learn for the week. But Starr is in a hurry, and doesn't correctly spell the last word, which Sage hears as *Miss Alaineus*. Sage's mistake causes her great embarrassment when she returns to school, but she makes up for it in the vocabulary parade, where she dresses as "Miss Alaineus: Queen of All Miscellaneous Things" and wins a gold trophy for "The Most Original Use of a Word."

Although *Miss Alaineus* is a lighthearted and clever picture book about mistaken vocabulary words and the power of children's resilience, we do not recommend using it as a model for vocabulary instruction. In the book, Sage's main experience with vocabulary (until the delightful word parade at the end) is writing dictionary definitions and sentences related to a theme. To us, the book demonstrates the pitfalls of assigning word lists without also giving students engaging experiences with vocabulary. However, *Miss Alaineus* does illustrate a common problem when teaching vocabulary. That is, while students may have heard targeted words before encountering them in formal vocabulary instruction, they may also have misconceptions about the word meanings, pronunciations, or spellings. Lacking full understanding they may not use the words accurately or, perhaps, at all. Indeed, vocabulary mishaps can eventually lead to knowledge gaps in science, mathematics, and other content areas.

We read *Miss Alaineus* to our students because the book is a fun way to discuss vocabulary, but afterward we share our own misunderstandings and explain how we have dealt with the ensuing problems. We use these stories to let students know that we all have to learn from our mistakes and that talking about vocabulary can help us clear up misconceptions.

With the implementation of the Common Core State Standards, there will certainly be higher expectations for students to learn grade-appropriate vocabulary, and our instruction will need to be intentional and intensive if we hope to guide them well. In previous chapters, we described our plan for incorporating strategic vocabulary instruction. In this chapter, we share additional classroom activities that will deepen students' word knowledge.

Extending Vocabulary Through Morphology

We know that morphemic awareness can increase students' literacy success (Carlisle et al. 2010). Proficient readers usually have learned how to use prefixes, suffixes, and Greek and Latin roots to understand word relationships and decipher longer, unfamiliar words. Most linguists agree that Greek- and Latin-derived words comprise a good percentage of the words used in English texts (Moats 2000; Templeton et al. 2010), with some estimates as high as 60 percent.

The ability to use affixes (prefixes, suffixes, and inflectional endings) to determine the meanings of unknown words is now part of the Common Core State Standards as early as kindergarten (L.K.4b). By grade two, students are expected to "use a known root word as a clue to the meaning of an unknown word with the same root (e.g., *addition, additional*)" (L.2.4c). By fourth grade, one of the standards is "Use common grade-appropriate Greek and Latin affixes and roots as clues to the meaning of a word" (L.4.4b).

To foster morphemic awareness, we teach our intermediate students how to confidently tackle the multisyllabic vocabulary they encounter in core academic courses. We want them to be inspired by the challenge of figuring out "big words" instead of being so intimidated that they shut down and stop trying. Preparing students for sophisticated word study represents a huge shift in expectations for children who are at risk of failing in school because of their poor preparation for learning. It says they are capable of getting on track for college by making an easier transition to the mostly expository reading that is emphasized at the secondary level.

We start with some of the most common Greek and Latin roots to help students enhance word schema and enlarge their vocabularies as they learn how words are related. We also teach students the meanings of the most common prefixes, such as *un-, re-, dis-, in-, im-, il-,* and *-ir,* the most common suffixes, such as *-able/-ible, -ly, -ness,* and *-tion,* and the spelling changes associated with the addition of inflections beginning with vowels, such as *-es, -ed,* and *-ing.* When our students know the meanings of the most common word parts, they gain the vocabulary power to successfully analyze the meanings of literally hundreds of new printed words.

One of our favorite resources is *Cryptomania! Teleporting into Greek and Latin with the CryptoKids* (Fine 2004). This ideal picture book is jam-packed with morphological information. We use a book talk to introduce *Cryptomania!* and then focus on a section, "Calling All Cryptokids," which we project onto the document camera so the entire class can see the page. Later, we place *Cryptomania!* in the classroom library and invite students to explore the book during their self-selected reading time. It's not uncommon to see students poring over pictures and text in the book, making connections to words they have already added to their word banks.

Crystal Ball Words

After our students have participated in several weeks of discussion about the meaning of prefixes and suffixes and have learned a few Greek and Latin roots, we use an activity called Crystal Ball Words to begin our study of morphology. The name comes from our playful way of encouraging students to look deeply into a word to predict its meaning. Leslie and Brenda created a three-column graphic organizer (see Figure 7.1 and Appendix G) to help students brainstorm words that share Greek or Latin roots. Using the graphic organizer, students can quickly see how the prefixes, roots, and suffixes provide clues to the meanings of multisyllabic words.

Transportation is the word Leslie has chosen to display on the document camera at the beginning of today's vocabulary lesson. "We are going to infer the meaning of this word from what you already know," she tells her fourth graders. "Look at the part of the word

Name:_____   Date:_____

Crystal Ball Words

WORD:		
Prefix:	Root:	Suffix:
Prefix definition:	Root definition:	Suffix definition:
Other words with this prefix:	Other words with this root:	Other words with this suffix:

Look deep into a word to predict its meaning.

Figure 7.1 *Graphic organizer for Crystal Ball Words*

transportation that says *trans-*, which is a prefix that means 'across.' We are going to think of some words that includes the word part *trans-*."

She points to the middle of the word. "Now let's look at *port*. *Port* was one of your vocabulary words. Do you remember what it means?"

"It means a place where boats can be safe," Davion answers.

"Right. But it has another meaning," Leslie says. "In Latin, *port* means 'to carry.' We are also going to think about bigger words that have the little word *port* in them."

Pointing to the end of the word, Leslie says, "I know you know what the suffix *-tion* means. We've studied it before."

Alexa says, "I know! It means 'act or process of.' "

"Is it that way even if that *a* is there?" asks David, eyeing the suffix *-ation*.

Leslie answers, "Good question! Yes, they mean the same."

Heads nod; this explanation makes sense to them.

"Okay," Leslie says, "So *transportation* means 'the act or process of carrying across.' What kinds of vehicles carry things, and what kinds of things do they carry?"

Students brainstorm and come up with: a boat that carries cargo across water, a plane that carries people and cargo across the air, a car that carries people across the country, a bike that can carry a person across the park, and a helicopter that can carry people across the city. Leslie asks for earlier forms of vehicles, and students also add a horse, a carriage, and a donkey to the list.

Leslie reminds her students that *trans-* means "across or through." She then asks them to brainstorm words they have heard that contain the prefix *trans-*. As they call out words, Leslie writes the suggestions on the projected graphic organizer, and students do the same on the printed versions at their desks (see Figure 7.2). Some of the suggestions are words that students have learned during previous vocabulary lessons. Some are words they may have heard but can't define. Leslie and her students discuss how the prefix *trans-* contributes to the meaning of various words. For example, *transcribe* means "to write across languages, or to translate," *transatlantic* means "across the Atlantic Ocean," and *transparent* means "perfectly clear or obvious; light shows clearly through."

When they move to the next column on the graphic organizer and see the root word *port,* the kids begin to get excited.

"We live in Portland!" Tayaunna exclaims, referring to the neighborhood of Louisville where the school is located.

"Well, yes we do! So what does the word *Portland* mean?" Leslie asks. After some discussion, the students realize that Portland's name came from the neighborhood's proximity to a cargo dock along the Ohio River.

"That's cool!" exclaims Michael.

"I never knew that!" adds Tasha.

"Hey, I know another one—airport!" Lawrence says, returning to the earlier discussion about words with the same root. "Planes carry stuff."

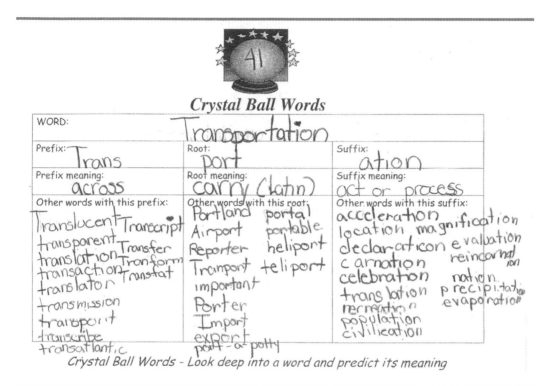

Crystal Ball Words - Look deep into a word and predict its meaning

Figure 7.2 *A student's completed graphic organizer for the word* transportation

"Good connections—keep them coming," Leslie encourages, and hands shoot up as students call out:

"Reporter!"

"Important!"

"Support!"

"Portable!"

Their favorite word is the brand name *Porta-potty.*

"Hey, that means you can carry your potty!" Kevan says, and everyone joins in laughing.

When Leslie's students get to the suffix *-ation*, they come up with a list that includes *acceleration* (the act or process of accelerating), *location* (the act or process of locating), and *destination* (the act or process of getting to your destiny). Students also add many words they have learned in science, such as *condensation*, *evaporation*, and *precipitation*. Leslie helps them look at the word parts to determine the meanings. At the end of the lesson, she asks, "So, how many words were we able to discover in just one Crystal Ball Word?"

Students count, and then call excitedly, "Forty-one!" Leslie reinforces their learning by saying, "So, from one word you discovered that you really know forty-one words! I'd love to know if you find any of these words or even more with these parts while you are reading this week." They write the number 41 in the middle of the crystal ball icon on their graphic organizers and close their folders. In the following weeks, when students review their vocabulary resources, Leslie will listen for the application of words students have brainstormed today.

Leslie's fourth graders gained such confidence applying their morphemic awareness that she made Crystal Ball Wednesdays a regular part of her vocabulary routine. But Leslie also had some missteps along the way, and she urges other teachers to carefully consider the words they plan to review each week.

"The first time I did this activity I chose the word *prediction*," Leslie recalled. "I thought it would be a great word to begin with since we were introducing the Crystal Ball Word activity."

Fourth graders being fourth graders, they could not stop giggling about the root word, and all serious study ended almost as soon as it had started. "As you can imagine, I had to start over with another word," Leslie says, shaking her head ruefully. "Later, when they were used to the activity, I could go back to the word *prediction*."

Other times, however, adolescent humor can be just the right ingredient for a morphology lesson. The year Margot was teaching fourth grade, she also engaged her students in the study of morphology. One day her students were reading a text selection that included the word *termination*. Kids looked puzzled as they tried to determine the meaning of the word. All of a sudden, Samuel brightened. "Hey, like *The Terminator*," he said, making a connection to the movie starring Arnold Schwarzenegger.

Margot chuckled. "So, what does The Terminator do?"

Michael called out, "He kills people!" All the students laughed (gruesome, yes, but they *are* fourth graders). Encouraged, Michael added in his best Schwarzenegger-like swagger, "I'll be back!"

"Okay, okay. Let's think about the word for a minute," said Margot. "What is the meaning of the suffix at the end of the word?"

"The act or process of!" chimed the class.

"Great. And what does the root *term* mean?"

Dariah stepped over to the computer and did a quick Internet search for the root word. "It means 'a fixed time,'" she read aloud.

Margot led them further. "What happens after a fixed time?"

"I guess it's the end," said Thaddius.

"Right," said Margot. "And we've had the antonym in vocabulary. Does anyone remember the antonym of the word *origin*?"

"One antonym is *finish*," said Serena. "Ohhh! I know! The Terminator finishes people!" The rest of the students looked wide-eyed as they got the connection.

"So, *termination* means . . ." Margot said, looking around the classroom.

"The act or process of finishing," Michael announced triumphantly.

And just like that, a formerly difficult word became a cherished class memory—and the latest addition to the students' vocabulary bank.

Background Knowledge and Comprehension Instruction

Proficient readers automatically use context clues to connect the text with their background knowledge, or what they already know about the topic. This activates schema and helps readers comprehend the text. As Ellin Keene and Susan Zimmermann suggest in *Mosaic of Thought* (1997), when we teach comprehension strategy lessons we often ask our students to make three types of connections: text-to-self, text-to-text, and text-to-world.

Over the years, we have realized that our students have plenty of experience in their own neighborhoods, but often have a difficult time looking beyond their own horizons to the real and imagined worlds that authors portray to make a text-to-world connection. This is another reason we believe that explicit and deep vocabulary instruction is crucial for children of poverty. They need rich and varied experiences with words to call on when trying to comprehend new texts. Learning historical and cultural contexts of new words, for example, colors definitions in particularly vibrant ways.

Consider the day Leslie's fourth-grade class read a short biography about Samuel Goldwyn, the famous movie producer. Part of the story recounted how Goldwyn traveled to the United States when he was young and penniless to make a better life for himself. While discussing the text, Leslie asked, "Can any of you make a connection to this story?"

She expected to hear her students relate personal experiences having to do with "being penniless" or the time they had watched an old movie on television. Instead, she was delighted when T.J. exclaimed, "I have a text-to-world connection! It reminds me of the immigrants, pioneers, and explorers because they were looking for a better life in a new land."

T.J. was quite proud of his insight, but we were just as excited because of the reason he could make that strong text-to-world connection. *Immigrant*, *pioneer*, and *explorer* were all words he had learned during vocabulary instruction. The enormous cognitive leap that T.J. made while reading about Samuel Goldwyn's life gave us reason to hope that other vocabulary lessons would inspire students to make similar comprehension connections. As Leslie says, "It made my job that much more significant because I realized I am not just teaching my kids about vocabulary—I am really teaching them about the world."

Inference and Vocabulary

Engaging students in activities that ask them to apply vocabulary improves their comprehension and helps them recognize vocabulary as a fluid and standard component of academic conversations rather than just a list of words on an anchor chart. The students from both classes were gathered in Margot's room one day when Brenda held up a copy of *Grandfather's Journey* by Allen Say (1993). She had chosen this book not only because the content related to immigration, which was part of their social studies theme, but also because of the use of inference required for comprehension. At first glance, *Grandfather's Journey* seems to be a simple story of a Japanese immigrant's journey to the United States in the early twentieth century and his resulting love of both countries. But the sparse text belies the complexity of the book. There are numerous text-to-world connections that students must make in order to comprehend the author's message.

Consider the following passage:

But a war began. Bombs fell from the sky and scattered our lives like leaves in a storm. (Say 1993)

As they follow the text, proficient readers ask themselves clarifying questions such as: *What war started? What country is this? What do I know about wars that have occurred in the past? What do I know about the ways in which bombs have affected people's lives?* Drawing on life experience and background knowledge when reading the book, adults would likely realize that the author is referring to Pearl Harbor, World War II, or the nuclear bombs that destroyed Hiroshima and Nagasaki. We may draw conclusions about the text that children cannot do simply because we have more context for understanding.

Before reading *Grandfather's Journey*, we prepared our students by teaching them how to draw conclusions and make inferences using a graphic organizer and the following equation:

Clues from the Text + What I Already Know = Inference or Conclusion

We also taught them to provide textual evidence to support their conclusions by quoting the text. The students had used this equation for several previous reading comprehension lessons, but on this day we wanted them to add vocabulary words to make connections that would fit in the equation.

Margot used a document camera to project the cover of *Grandfather's Journey* as Brenda said, "When you make a prediction you are inferring. We might infer from the cover illustration and the title what the book is about. What predictions can you make about *Grandfather's Journey* just from the cover and the title? Please take a minute to discuss with your group."

Shamyia, Dell, Marcus, and Jaydin were seated together and had this conversation:

Jaydin:	I think it is probably about a grandfather going all around the world by himself.
Marcus:	And maybe he traveled through the water and went on airplanes.
Dell:	There is going to be travel for sure.
Marcus:	He could be a traveler, or a settler, or an ancestor.

Although the students didn't know it, Marcus had already moved into the next part of the activity. *Settler* and *ancestor* were vocabulary words the class had studied and Marcus had applied these terms to the task. Following up on their predictions, Brenda pointed out the students' use of vocabulary within their small-group discussions.

Brenda next read the book aloud, stopping periodically to encourage students to make connections to the text. After a brief discussion of the story, she gave each student a typed copy of a few pages of the text and a blank copy of the graphic organizer (see Figure 7.3).

"Start with the first sentence," Brenda said. "Your job is to work with your group and use the graphic organizer to decide: What are context clues in the sentence that help you decide the author's meaning? What background knowledge do you have about the sentence? What conclusions can you draw or inferences can you make? And if you can, use vocabulary you have learned to make your connections."

Shamyia, Dell, Marcus, and Jaydin continued to work together to carry out the assignment.

Marcus:	Okay, the first sentence is, "My grandfather was a young man when he left his home in Japan and went to see the world."
Dell:	I'll write it in the first box.

Grandfather's Journey

Clues from the Text	What I Already Know (Background Knowledge)	My Inference/Conclusion
"My grandfather was a young man when he left his home in Japan and went to see the world."	Grandfather was a immagrant. I can relate to the story 2 homes because both characters from the story were wanting to see the world.	I can conclude that grandfather was aventurous, and brave because he left Japan to see the world.
"The endless farm feilds reminded him of the ocean he had crossed"	I can make a text self connect because me and my family travel to califoria to the ocean and took a cruise.	I can conclude that grandfather was suprise because he was in a new country and was exploring the world that he never seen before.
"He met many people along the way. He shook hands with black men and white men, with yellow men and red men."	I can make a connect to Martin L. King Jr. he didn't care about race he was just normal.	I can conclude that grandfather was respectful and didn't care about race.

Figure 7.3 *Inference chart for* Grandfather's Journey *(Say 1993)*

Shamyia:	If this is a sentence from the text, we need to put quotation marks around it.
Dell:	But no one's talking.
Shamyia:	I know, but we are quoting words from the story. Remember?
Dell:	Oh, yeah.
Marcus:	Well, my background knowledge is he was a young man.
Jaydin:	Why did he leave?
Marcus:	The last part actually tells you why he left. That's an important part.
Dell:	He wanted to see what the world looked like. That's what he wanted!
Jaydin:	Maybe he wanted to see different cultures.
Marcus:	I think he was an immigrant.
Shamyia:	You know what? We have background knowledge to the story *Two Homes*, because some of the characters in there were immigrants.
Marcus:	Hey! You just made a text-to-text connection!
Dell:	Like Grandfather wanted to see how different other cultures were from Japan.
Jaydin:	So he wanted to compare the countries.
Shamyia:	It's also like the story *Family Treasures*. That person in that story wanted to see the world just like Grandfather.
Marcus:	I think Grandfather was an immigrant! He wanted to see what the world is like. That's the whole point!

For this sentence, Dell wrote:

In the Book: *"My grandfather was a young man when he left his home in Japan and went to see the world."*

This Reminds Me Of . . . : *This reminds me of the story* Two Homes *because there were immigrants in that story too.*

New Idea or Conclusion: *Grandfather was an immigrant. He wanted to see what the world was like.*

As they discussed the story, this group of students used the vocabulary words *immigrant*, *culture*, and *compare* to make text-to-world connections. In his writing about background knowledge, Dell also made a text-to-text connection to another story, used the vocabulary word *immigrant*, and incorporated that same word into his conclusion.

When we reviewed Shamyia's completed graphic organizer for vocabulary use, we found that she likewise made connections to appropriate background knowledge, made logical inferences, and made text-to-text connections. In addition, she used the words *curious*, *destination*, *cautious*, and *determined*, all of which had either been vocabulary words or synonyms or antonyms for those terms sometime during the school year and several of which represented text-to-world connections for Shamyia.

Extending Vocabulary Development with Children's Literature

Many authors have written about using picture books—a brief text with illustrations that help tell a story—as a bridge to teaching reading comprehension strategies. In *Strategies That Work*, for example, Stephanie Harvey and Anne Goudvis (2007) consider picture books strong choices for comprehension lessons because of their brevity, clarity of message, and outstanding artwork to enrich the text. In their book about critical literacy strategies to enhance student comprehension, Maureen McLaughlin and Glen DeVoogd (2004) also recommend using picture books for all grade levels to teach students how to analyze the author's message.

Bill Bintz and Sara Moore (2002) have found that analyzing picture books for their "text potential," or their ability to help students understand concepts inferred in the book, can also be valuable in extending content-area instruction at the secondary level. For example, the authors use books such as *Snowflake Bentley* (Martin 1989) and *Starry Messenger: Galileo Galilei* (Sis 2000) as a text set to teach inquiry in middle school science.

As the old saying goes, a picture is worth a thousand words. Picture books and other examples of children's literature that are rich in vocabulary can become exceptional tools for student learning. Remembering the Hayes and Ahrens (1988) research about the high number of rare words in much of children's literature (discussed in Chapter 1), we often incorporate picture books into our vocabulary instruction.

For example, Lemony Snicket (the pen name of Daniel Handler) is the author of the popular children's book series entitled A Series of Unfortunate Events, as well as several picture books, including *13 Words*. Snicket is a vocabulary teacher's dream—a master of the embedded definition and witty turn of phrase. To parody Snicket, the words *embedded definition* here mean "when an author explains the definition of a word right in the sentence so you don't have to look it up in a dusty dictionary." Snicket loves to play with language, using a plethora of Latin-based words and literacy references, and his writing has great potential for vocabulary development (Arter and Nilsen 2009).

We have already discussed two learning experiences that began with picture books and ended with extending our students' vocabulary development. In the rest of this chapter, we will discuss the text potential of other books to help students think more deeply about vocabulary connections and enhance vocabulary knowledge.

Extending Oral Language Development

When Brenda saw the book *Pirate Pete's Talk Like a Pirate* (Kennedy 2007) in a local bookstore, she couldn't wait to take it back to Atkinson. In this delightful book, Pirate Pete is searching for a crew. He stipulates that a crew member must talk like a pirate, with plenty of "Aarrgh's" and rustic, salty-dog language. As he approaches Rascal Island, Pirate Pete just knows he will find his crew. But to his dismay, it turns out that Rascals speak in a very different manner! Here is an example from one page:

> Pirate Pete: *Is ye brave? 'Cause no lily-livered seafarer is gonna sail with me!*
>
> Rascal: *I can assure you that I am extremely courageous. I will conduct myself with valor at all times.*
>
> Pirate Pete: *Confound it! Ye don't talk like a pirate! Walk the plank!*

Talk Like a Pirate is full of attention-grabbing words, with a tongue-in-cheek attitude about elegant language and vocabulary. As we read *Talk Like a Pirate*, we discussed the book's text potential and thought about how we might use this book to further our students' vocabulary learning. Although we were tempted to use vocabulary words having to do with pirates (which would not advance our curriculum) or just teach the interesting words in the book (which were not connected with our content), we thought the book had more text potential for vocabulary instruction and decided to go with a broader idea. We taught vocabulary words aligned with the fourth-grade social studies curriculum, but we also gave our students an opportunity to apply these words in a fun, thematic way. After reading *Talk Like a Pirate* aloud to the class, we helped our students learn to transform what we called "pirate talk"—using basic words and sentences—into "rascal talk," which would be more sophisticated, expressive sentences using their vocabulary words.

Talking Like Rascals

On this day the fourth-grade words are: *swift, analyze, model, currents, coastline, visible, shore, chisel,* and *wedge.* Through the strategic vocabulary routine, students have already explored most of these words from the science and social studies curriculum. Leslie used the pocket chart, the class added synonyms and antonyms, and students completed journal entries for all the words. Leslie also read aloud *Pirate Pete's Talk Like a Pirate,* and the kids laughed about talking like pirates and rascals.

Today Leslie has prepared index cards with "pirate talk" sentences, which are rudimentary sentences such as "Me can't see stuff far away." She prepared these cards herself because she did not want her students to practice writing pirate talk. "They already know how to speak pirate well enough!" she chuckles.

Students sit with partners. Leslie gives each pair of students one of the pirate sentence cards and a blank card. She explains that their task is to turn the pirate sentence into a rascal sentence—that is, a sophisticated sentence using one or more of the vocabulary words. Leslie reminds students they can use their vocabulary journals to do this task and that a rascal would probably use a 7-Up sentence.

Dasia and Tony are partners. Their pirate sentence card says, "Me cut rock with me tool."

Tony announces, "I can do this one. The word is *chisel*. We could say 'I cut a rock with my chisel.'"

Dasia looks puzzled. "I can't remember. What exactly is a chisel?"

Tony answers, "It's a tool to cut a rock."

"Oh, yeah, I remember now," says Dasia. "What about this: 'I cut the rock with a chisel and with my tool'?"

"That's not rascal talk. And a chisel *is* a tool," replies Tony. "How about, 'I cut the rock with a chisel that is very sharp'?"

Dasia looks unconvinced. "You won't be able to fit that on the card, and it might not sound right."

"What would be a good word to go with chisel?" counters Tony.

Leslie has been listening to the discussion. She leans in toward Tony and Dasia and says, "You really need to dazzle it up. That's how a rascal would talk."

Tony brightens. "I know! 'My chisel blazes through a rock!'"

Leslie looks delighted. "I like the way you are headed!"

Dasia tries it out on her paper. "My chisel bladed . . ."

"Blazes," corrects Tony.

"What does that even mean?" asks Dasia.

Tony jumps up and acts like he is using a chisel on a rock, really putting some muscle into it. "I'm doing it now."

Dasia whispers as she writes on the card, "My chisel bladed—no, blazes—through the rock," and then adds aloud excitedly, "like a swift runner!"

Tony exclaims, "That's good! You used another vocabulary word, too! How many words does it have now?"

Dasia counts. "Ten! Let's make another one!"

"Cool!" says Tony. He starts another sentence. "I cut the rock with my hammer and chisel."

"That sounds like the last sentence," chides Dasia. "We have to be different."

Tony tries again. "The chisel was difficult to break."

Dasia looks perplexed. "Why would you want to break the chisel?"

They think. Dasia then says, "I know! 'I hit the chisel so hard that it almost demolished and made the earth quiver.'"

"Hey, yeah! That's great! Write that down!" exclaims Tony, with satisfaction.

At a signal from Leslie, students trade pirate talk cards so they can work on creating a new rascal sentence. The conversation about how to transform pirate talk into rascal talk continues as students create new cards.

Pirate Party

To celebrate and review the vocabulary words from our pirate vocabulary cycle, Leslie plans a Pirate Party. She places students in groups of four. Each student wears an eye patch made of black construction paper and red string, with a skull and crossbones symbol drawn in chalk (see Figure 7.4). A pirate booty chest (a small cardboard treasure chest easily found in the birthday party aisle at discount and party supply stores) holding a supply of gleaming plastic gold coins sits in front of each group of four students.

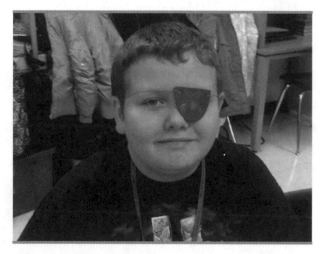

Figure 7.4 *David wears an eye patch during the Pirate Party.*

During the celebration, the students play a game we call Talk Like a Rascal. Leslie has set up the *Eggspert* game system and holds a stack of index cards, each with one of the pirate sentences the students had worked with in their partner activity the week before. Leslie calls one student from each group to come to the front and hold an *Eggspert* buzzer, primed to be the first person to answer.

Leslie reads the first pirate sentence, "Me see me small ship." Students buzz in, eager to turn this pirate sentence into a rascal sentence.

Tomias edges out the others as his green buzzer flashes. Leslie acknowledges him as the first to answer. "My miniscule model ship was visible on the table!" he says triumphantly. Leslie proclaims that this is indeed a rascal sentence that could be made from the pirate sentence, and Tomias struts back to his group. As the winners of the round, the members of Tomias's group each put a gold coin into their treasure chest. The five other students who do not win this round then line up to "walk the plank,"—a two-by-four-foot board that Leslie had pulled from beneath her bed and placed on the floor of her classroom. While each giggling student walks the plank, the other members of the class growl, "Aargh!" in their best pirate voices. At the end of the game, the students in the group with the most gold coins choose a prize from a collection of pirate-themed birthday party souvenirs. They beg Leslie to have another vocabulary Pirate Party soon.

An ultimate goal of the Common Core State Standards is for students to be able to "acquire and use accurately a range of general academic and domain-specific words and phrases sufficient for reading, writing, speaking, and listening . . ." (CCR.L.6). Using *Pirate Pete's Talk Like a Pirate*, we expanded a basic vocabulary lesson and showed students the power of expressive language using academic and domain-specific vocabulary.

More Books to Extend Vocabulary Learning

It is not difficult to find examples of nonfiction picture books appropriate for vocabulary study. Simply ask a library/media specialist for help or search the Internet and you will find recommended lists related to almost any content area. An excellent annotated bibliography of "Great Books for Teaching Content" can be found in Appendix A of *Strategies That Work*, second edition (Harvey and Goudvis 2007). Because it is so easy to find and use nonfiction trade books for vocabulary development of content words, we have instead chosen to suggest examples of children's fiction that could be used as part of vocabulary instruction. We offer the following books as possibilities for class read-alouds or independent reading. Suggestions for related vocabulary lessons are included.

13 Words

Author: Lemony Snicket
Illustrator: Maira Kalman
Publisher: HarperCollins (2010)
In this book, Snicket has chosen thirteen unrelated words—*bird, despondent, cake, dog, busy, convertible, goat, hat, haberdashery, scarlet, baby, panache*, and *mezzo-soprano* —and linked them together into a wacky story. The text is peppered with other interesting words, such as *spiffy, verve, swagger*, and *pensive*.

After sharing *13 Words* (and the highly amusing book trailer at Lemony Snicket's website at www.lemonysnicket.com), ask students to work with partners and use thirteen vocabulary words (or interesting words they have found in the dictionary) to write a wacky story in the manner of Lemony Snicket. Using another author's pattern as a framework for students' own writing is called "copy change" (Bintz, Wright, and Sheffer 2010). In the case of Lemony Snicket, students can "copy-change" his style of linking words that don't seem related and embedding the definitions of vocabulary words. Writing a story linking interesting words is yet another way for students to develop word networks, and embedding definitions requires them to ponder the meaning of the word in that particular context. For a further extension, students can create their own story trailers by using simple digital storytelling tools, such as Photo Story or Animoto.

A River of Words:
The Story of William Carlos Williams

Author: Jen Bryant
Illustrator: Melissa Sweet
Publisher: Eerdmans Books for Young Readers (2008)

A River of Words is a Caldecott Honor book about the life of the American poet William Carlos Williams and how he fulfilled his dream of writing poetry, even as he became a busy family doctor. The book includes examples of Williams's early drafts; it becomes clear that even though his poetry is deceptively simple, Williams selected each word with care to create imagery in readers' minds.

After reading aloud *A River of Words* and discussing the book, place students in small groups and ask them to choose one of their vocabulary words. Each group can then create a concept map with a circle in the middle containing the vocabulary word and then brainstorm related visual and sensory images and words. (Basic concept map templates can be found online at sites such as www.readingrockets. org/strategies/concept_maps/.) For example, what would words such as *vast*, *reflection*, or *circuit* look like, sound like, smell like, taste like, or feel like? What other word relationships can they identify? What do they see in their minds when they think about the words? Students can also use the concept map to write simple poems about the group's vocabulary word. This activity will help students build word schema and strengthen memory.

Baloney, Henry P.

Author: Jon Scieszka
Illustrator: Lane Smith
Publisher: Viking (2001)

Henry P. Baloney is a boy in space who has to come up with a reason for being late for school or his teacher, Miss Bugscuffle, will assign him Permanent Lifelong Detention. Henry proceeds to tell the story of why he is late to *szkola*—because he misplaced his trusty *zimulis*. The story becomes wilder and wilder as he describes his astronomical adventures, all the while inserting words that sound like nonsense. At the end of the book, the author explains that the story is actually written in a combination of words from different languages, and a decoder gives the translations.

Baloney, Henry P. could be used as a springboard to vocabulary study (author Jon Scieszka *loves* to play with language) and learning words through context. First, read the book aloud to students without showing the pictures. Next, discuss how the interesting words come from different languages. Give students a typed copy of the story with a few of the unfamiliar words underlined or in boldface and then allow them to work in groups to think about a possible meaning for each of the designated words. Students will have to work hard to use sentence-level and passage-level context clues to decide possible meanings. For example, *szkola* means "school" in Polish and *zimulis* is Latvian for "pencil." In the text, there are immediate obvious clues for the meaning of *szkola*, while it usually takes more clues and more experiences with the text to figure out the meaning of *zimulis*. Discuss students' choices of word meanings, and then read the story aloud again and show the pictures so students can decide if they were right. Make sure to ask students to explain the context clues that helped them predict the meaning of the words. Help students make connections between using context clues for word meaning in the story and using context clues to determine word meaning in other texts. *Baloney, Henry P.* can become a touchstone text for the use of context clues, as you refer to it again and again during vocabulary instruction.

Detective LaRue: Letters from the Investigation

Author: Mark Teague
Illustrator: Mark Teague
Publisher: Scholastic (2004)

This book is one of several by Mark Teague about Ike LaRue, the writing dog. In *Letters from the Investigation*, Ike, Mrs. LaRue's dog, has been accused of a horrible crime. A neighbor's cats are missing, and it seems that Ike may be the culprit. Ike is taken to the police station for questioning (a really nice police station where he eats donuts, plays card games with the officers, and uses a typewriter at a desk), and he begins writing to Mrs. LaRue to tell his wildly exaggerated side of the story. In a series of letters, Ike tells her that he has been wronged but has escaped from jail and is searching for the cats. He further tells her that now he must remain in hiding, saying, "It is a situation rife with intrigue and danger" (in reality, he is staying at the Plaza Hotel and attending a baseball game). The book contains an abundance of descriptive adjectives, adverbs, and strong nouns and verbs, such as *intrepid, apparently, sleuth, heroism,* and *speculated.* News clippings from the hilarious *Snort City*

Register are interspersed and help to fill in some of the detail of the story. Ike turns out to be a hero in the end when he accidentally rescues two "canary burglars" who look suspiciously like the cats that were missing.

After reading aloud *Detective LaRue: Letters from the Investigation,* teach your students the parts of a friendly letter. Arrange students into partners. Students will choose vocabulary words and write a brief letter to their partners trying to persuade them of the importance of their words. Students should state an opinion in their letters and supply at least three reasons to support the opinion. They should also have access to a thesaurus so they can add juicy nouns, verbs, adjectives, and adverbs to their writing. Students can then exchange letters and write a reply explaining whether they thought their partner's letter was convincing and interesting, providing reasons and evidence about why they will or will not use the partner's word in the future.

Donovan's Word Jar

Author: Monalisa DeGross
Illustrator: Cheryl Hanna
Publisher: Amistad (1998)

All of Donovan's friends collect things, so he starts a collection of his own—interesting words he writes on slips of paper and puts in a jar. Along the way, he describes why he likes the words he finds. When the jar gets too full, Donovan has a dilemma. What should he do with all the words? He ends up sharing them with his grandmother and her friends, and then he starts filling another jar with words.

Donovan's Word Jar is a very short chapter book that can be used as a read-aloud with a class, requiring just a few minutes each day. Afterward, give students plastic bags with several slips of paper, and ask them to collect their own fascinating words for a class word jar. Make sure they write their names on the back of each word. Pull a few words from the jar each day and talk about the meaning of the word and how it might be used (Allen and Gonzalez 1998). Using the document camera, ask the kids to help sort the words into categories—parts of speech, content areas, or words that sound juicy—and then post them on a bulletin board or anchor chart. The purpose is to create "word consciousness" as part of a classroom community focused on vocabulary.

Frindle

Author: Andrew Clements
Illustrator: Brian Selznick
Publisher: Atheneum (1996)

Frindle is a brief chapter book about Nick Allen, a creative fifth-grade boy who loves to energize school. However, he meets his match with his new teacher, Mrs. Granger, who insists that her students spend time using the dictionary to learn vocabulary. Nick immediately gets into trouble with Mrs. Granger, and she requires him to do a report about the dictionary where he learns how words are added to the English language. To retaliate against Mrs. Granger, Nick decides to begin calling a pen a "frindle" and encouraging the other kids to do the same. The situation spins out of control as *frindle* catches on across the school and beyond. *Frindle* has an unexpected ending that will help students understand the importance of the dictionary.

In *Frindle*, Nick created a new word, but there are also many unfamiliar real words in the dictionary. After reading and allowing students to discuss the book, ask them to use a dictionary to choose and study a thought-provoking word that is unfamiliar to them. Then ask students to use their word throughout the week and see if they can get others to use it, too. Hold a *Frindle* Week on a regular basis so that kids get a chance to try out an assortment of new words. A great tool for students to keep track of words they find is the Vocabulary Bookmark found on the Scholastic website at http://printables.scholastic.com/printables/detail/?id=35602.

June 29, 1999

Author: David Weisner
Illustrator: David Weisner
Publisher: Clarion Books (1992)

On June 29, 1999, in Ho-Ho-Kus, New Jersey, Holly Evans, a young girl working on a class science project, launches vegetable seedlings into the ionosphere. Holly intends to "study the effects of extraterrestrial conditions on vegetable growth and development." A few weeks later, giant vegetables begin landing on earth. TV stations broadcast twenty-four-hour news of the "airborne vegetal event." The enormous vegetables cause a chain of events affecting trade, real estate, tourism, and the economy. Spinach blankets Greenwich, and arugula covers Ashtabula. There is just one problem—arugula was not part of Holly's experiment. Where did it come from?

June 29, 1999 is an imaginative picture book filled with thought-provoking vocabulary. In addition to providing an excellent example of how to follow a scientific process, the book contains references to social studies concepts that may be unfamiliar to many elementary students. This is a great text to teach inference, which is a building block of vocabulary knowledge and comprehension. What can we infer on each page? How do we use inference in vocabulary study?

Martin's Big Words:
The Life of Martin Luther King, Jr.

Author: Doreen Rappaport
Illustrator: Bryan Collier
Publisher: Hyperion Books (2001)

Martin's Big Words is a simple biography of Martin Luther King, Jr., with a compelling message about the power of words throughout his life. Many teachers already use this book to teach the concepts of civil rights and activism. To extend vocabulary development, ask students to choose previous vocabulary words that they consider powerful words that could change lives. Ask students to create and perform skits or develop a multimedia presentation to demonstrate the power of their chosen vocabulary words.

Max's Words

Author: Kate Banks
Illustrator: Boris Kulikov
Publisher: Farrar, Straus and Giroux (2006)

Max has two older brothers—one who collects coins and one who collects stamps. Max also wants a collection, so he begins to compile words cut out of magazines and newspapers. When Max realizes he can rearrange his words to create wondrous stories, his brothers envy Max's collection.

To promote word consciousness in your classroom, ask students to collect intriguing and unfamiliar vocabulary words and arrange them to create stories or poetry. Magnetic poetry kits are great tools for this. Students can also illustrate their writing for a "Class Words" display or a schoolwide demonstration.

The Boy Who Loved Words

Author: Roni Schotter
Illustrator: Giselle Potter
Publisher: Schwartz & Wade (2006)

The Boy Who Loved Words tells the story of Selig, who was a collector of words. Selig loved the sound (*tintinnabulating!*), taste (*tantalizing!*), and thought of words (*stirring* as they *percolated* in his brain). The illustrations show words floating in the background throughout much of this story as Selig savors language. Selig spends so much time collecting words that the other kids call him "Wordsworth" and tell him he is an *oddball*. Selig has a dream about a genie who tells him that he has a mission to distribute words. Selig accidentally helps a poet choose just the right words, and then continues to *disburse* words to assist others in knowing exactly the right word to say in different situations. One day, he hears a *mellifluous* note, and finds Melody, his true love. Together, they change the world. The endnotes of the book contain a glossary of all the words emphasized in the story.

The Boy Who Loved Words is another book that can be used as a springboard to vocabulary study. Teachers can read the story aloud once for student enjoyment, then read it again and ask students to predict the meaning of the highlighted words in context. *The Boy Who Loved Words* also has a strong message about choosing the right word for each situation. Ask students to point out places in the book where Selig helps people find just the right word, then guide students in a discussion about nuances in word meaning in different situations. Ask students to create illustrations of words that might describe the same thing but have a bit different meaning. For example, what would illustrations of the words *laugh*, *giggle*, and *guffaw* look like? In which contexts would each of the words be appropriate?

The Odious Ogre

Author: Norton Juster
Illustrator: Jules Feiffer
Publisher: Michael di Capua Books (2010)

The Odious Ogre roams the countryside terrorizing the citizens of the land and using quite an impressive vocabulary while he does so ("due mainly to having inadvertently swallowed a large dictionary while consuming the head librarian in one of the nearby towns"). He describes himself as "invulnerable, impregnable, insuperable, indefatigable, insurmountable." The Odious Ogre seems to be invincible, until he meets up with a young girl who is unimpressed and quite literally kills him with kindness.

The Odious Ogre contains a number of multisyllabic words that can help students increase morphemic awareness. Ask students to work in small groups to create and describe their own monster, using a dictionary to find impressive multisyllabic words to use in the description. Students can create and practice a skit about their monster, making sure to incorporate an assigned number of words that contain prefixes, suffixes, and if appropriate, Greek and Latin roots.

Chapter 8

Learning Through Assessment

Measurement is not to provide numbers but insight.
—Ingrid Bucher

In an era when high-stakes testing seems to dominate so many discussions about school success, one of our favorite picture books continues to be *Testing Miss Malarkey* (2003) by Judy Finchler. In the book, Miss Malarkey bites off her fingernails, Principal Wiggins loses his toupee, and all the other teachers are afflicted with vomiting fever when it becomes time to get ready for the "I.P.T.U." state test. In the meantime, the students notice that the teachers are acting very strangely and the cafeteria is only serving "brain food." Students are bewildered by the hubbub that surrounds test practice in every subject, from coloring circles with a number two pencil in art class to "becoming one with the test" in gym.

As teachers, we all have had the experience of taking a competitive standardized test, such as the SAT or GRE, which acts as a gatekeeper for the opportunities we will be afforded in the future. Many of these tests require sophisticated vocabulary knowledge to score well, making the stakes of word learning very high indeed.

High-stakes tests are often called assessments, but in reality assessment has a much broader role than fueling pressure in our academic lives. Every time we evaluate products or services, such as determining which apples look freshest at the supermarket (and in this example, we really *are* comparing apples to apples), we are assessing. Every time we collect data and attempt to develop an explanation for what we see, we are analyzing. Every time we observe patterns and habits and change or respond to them, we are adapting based on an assessment.

In the strategic vocabulary plan we follow at Atkinson, assessment plays a central part. Instruction would just be a collection of activities if we didn't pay close attention to how our kids are progressing and adjust accordingly. Formative vocabulary assessment is the glue that holds the pieces of our instruction together, and it helps us understand what our students actually know and can do. Summative assessment provides a record of vocabulary progress that we can report to administrators and parents. Yes, we must prepare our students for high-stakes assessments that the outside world will use to judge the success of our work in the classroom, but we also want our students to realize that assessment is a natural part of learning.

Planning Vocabulary Assessment

Research shows that teachers rarely assess vocabulary in a way that truly evaluates learning or use the results to help them plan further instruction. Andrew Biemiller, who has written extensively about vocabulary instruction, believes that one of the main reasons vocabulary assessment gets scant attention in the elementary grades is because there is insufficient knowledge about how to evaluate word knowledge (Biemiller 2004). Camille Blachowicz concurs, saying that we have "a clear vacuum in the research" about effective methods of assessing vocabulary (Blachowicz et al. 2006, 534). Nevertheless, we believe that research on effective measures of assessment generally can guide the development of better assessments specifically focused on vocabulary knowledge.

Because we have described our strategic vocabulary plan as a series of steps for each vocabulary cycle, it would be tempting to say that the last step is assessment. In reality, assessment is one of the first steps, one of the last steps, and part of everything we do in between. Being a good assessor is a lot like being a good doctor. When we evaluate students' vocabulary skills, we listen to the words they use and their misconceptions about words. We analyze student work, diagnose problem areas, review test results, and prescribe remedies. Regular and ongoing assessment helps us become highly aware of our students' progress in acquiring and using language, which in turn helps us develop a plan to address any vocabulary "ills."

We know we need to assess vocabulary progress in order to help our students develop their word learning, but how do we actually plan for vocabulary assessment? Rita Bean and Allison Swan Dagen, researchers in the field of literacy, have outlined four general guidelines to follow (Bean and Swan Dagen 2006). In the following paragraphs, we have boldfaced their guidelines and added our own thoughts about vocabulary assessment in our classrooms.

First, Bean and Swan Dagen urge teachers to **think about the *goals and purposes* of the assessment**. Is the objective to inform the public about vocabulary attainment, or is it to inform the teacher where she must reteach? In our classrooms, we believe there is a time and place for both actions as part of strategic vocabulary instruction. Summative assessment "sums up" the final outcome, and is more often used to inform the public. Formative assessment helps "form" our next steps in teaching.

Second, Bean and Swan Dagen suggest that **teachers should use *authentic measures* of vocabulary progress**. Such evaluations include observing students' vocabulary use, recording anecdotal notes, analyzing student work (including performances), and using other informal measures of student learning. Although we understand the need for formal summative assessment and develop and administer vocabulary tests in our classrooms, we believe that much vocabulary assessment can and should be done through informal measures that capture student knowledge throughout the school day.

Third, **teachers should plan for ways to assess** *depth of understanding*. Varied assessment tasks require different types of thinking and processing, from easy to more challenging. For formal assessments, we believe that students should experience tests that will eventually be used to judge them in the outside world. Thus, we use question formats found on standardized tests of vocabulary. For informal assessments, we want to measure depth of understanding by seeing what our students can do with words and how they are able to think about vocabulary every day.

Finally, Bean and Swan Dagen remind us that teachers should **be aware of** *comprehension connections* to vocabulary learning. We have found that sometimes a student knows how to decode and pronounce a word but doesn't know the meaning of that word. Sometimes a student only knows one definition of a word and then has trouble comprehending when the same word is used in another context. Sometimes a student can comprehend everything in a paragraph except one word, but that word is the key that unlocks the meaning of the passage. In all these cases, the student displays a comprehension problem that is really a lack of vocabulary knowledge.

Assessment in our strategic vocabulary plan involves a combination of all the components identified by Bean and Swan Dagen. We decide what to look for when students are engaged in vocabulary experiences and try to plan the kind of experiences that will reveal information about their progress. Reviewing evidence of student learning, such as tests and quizzes, student work, classroom conversations, and our observations, helps us identify gaps in knowledge. For students who need more attention, we add accommodations or supplementary experiences until we see that they are back on track for understanding the words and their applications. When we find gaps in vocabulary learning for the entire class, we reteach. When we find gaps in the progress of just a few students, we address it on a more individualized basis, such as during small-group guided reading.

In Figure 8.1, we have provided a vocabulary cycle plan with the learning experiences outlined in this book, their related assessments, and possible next steps in instruction. You will notice that most of the assessments are formative in nature. That is, we are gathering information about students' understanding so we can help them *before* giving a summative test for accountability purposes, such as a grade. Next, we will discuss the two major types of assessment in more detail.

Vocabulary Cycle Plan with Related Assessments		
Learning Experience	**Assessment**	**If Kids Need More . . .**
Day 1		
Word introduction	Teacher questioning; Thumbs Up/Thumbs Down to check understanding.	If most of group needs more instruction, reteach vocabulary words.
Student discussion	Observe by listening for use of vocabulary words.	Correct misconceptions through teacher questioning.
Begin journal entries	Observe journal entries to check for accurate application of words.	Quietly point out errors in spelling or word use. Correct misconceptions with individual students.
Day 2		
Add synonyms/ examples; antonyms/ non-examples	Observe efficient use of reference materials. Thumbs Up/Thumbs Down to check understanding of synonyms and antonyms.	Demonstrate use of reference materials. If most of group needs instruction, reteach synonyms/antonyms.
Student discussion	Observe by listening for accurate use of synonyms/ examples and antonyms/non-examples.	Correct misconceptions through teacher questioning.
Complete journal entries	Analyze journal entries for accuracy and misconceptions.	Correct misconceptions through further class discussion.
Scramble	Observe student positions to check for understanding of word relationships.	Correct misconceptions by repositioning students.
Possible Practice Activities **(5-Day Plan: Days 3–4/10-Day Plan: Days 3–9)**		
Counting Dude/ Bragging Dude	Observe to see if students can use the word in a sentence with seven or more words and understand word relationships with synonyms and antonyms.	Allow sentence starters. Correct misconceptions with individual students.
Vocabulary Rings	Analyze Vocabulary Ring cards for accuracy. Observe retrieval practice for ability to remember word meanings.	Try again.
Vocabulary Rap	Observe students for ability to name synonyms and antonyms fluently.	Repeat for fluency.

Figure 8.1 *Vocabulary Cycle Plan with related assessments*

Line It Up	Observe cards to see if students remember word meanings.	After discussing misconceptions, play game again. Pair struggling students with more capable peers.
Crystal Ball Words	Observe student discussion about meanings of parts of words.	Reteach meanings of word parts.
Word Charades	Observe for evidence of higher-level thinking about word meanings through drama.	Correct misconceptions through teacher and peer questioning. Ask students to try again.
Vocabulary Board Game	Observe by listening to student discussions. Analyze student-generated game questions for accuracy and application.	Correct misconceptions through teacher questioning.
Word Illustrations	Analyze word illustration drawings for evidence of higher-level thinking about word meanings through art.	Peers demonstrate successful illustrations. Ask students to try again.
Word Colors	Analyze word color cards for evidence of higher-level thinking about word meanings through art. Analyze explanations for color choices.	Peers demonstrate successful word color cards. Ask students to try again.
PowerPoint Portrayals	Analyze understanding of vocabulary word and related synonyms and antonyms through slides and verbal explanation.	Correct misconceptions through teacher and peer questioning.
Chain Link	Observe connections students make with words.	Revisit journal entries and try again.
5-Day Plan: Day 5/10-Day Plan: Day 10		
Celebration	Analyze student-generated game questions and/or discussion for mastery of word use.	Correct misconceptions through teacher questioning.
Teacher-Made Test	Analyze test for understanding of word meanings, application of words in context, and understanding of synonyms and antonyms.	Reteach words and word relationships in small group guided reading.

Figure 8.1 *continued*

Formative Assessment of Vocabulary Knowledge

At a recent holiday gathering, Brenda's three-year-old nephew, Lucas, ran up to her with an exciting question. "Do you know what *buoyant* means?" he asked. Without giving her time to respond, Lucas continued, "*Buoyant* means something can float." When Brenda asked if he could tell her about something that was buoyant, Lucas nodded and replied without hesitation, "Wood floats because it is buoyant. Because there is oxygen in it and oxygen makes the wood float." Satisfied that he had enlightened his aunt, Lucas then dashed off to play with his truck.

An informal assessment of this conversation could reveal several possibilities. First, Lucas is probably growing up in a highly literate environment where his parents and other adults are able to explain how the world works. Second, Lucas is remembering what he hears. At age three, he soaks up new vocabulary like a sponge, illuminating concepts he is curious about. Because he could remember and pronounce the word *buoyant* correctly, he had already stored the word in his working memory where he could retrieve it later. Third, Lucas could use *buoyant* in an appropriate context which had been explained to him. He is on his way to being able to apply the word in different situations as he learns more about the world. Fourth, it is hard not to compare Lucas's vocabulary progress with that of older children who do not come from such a vocabulary-enriched home environment. A quick and informal assessment has told us quite a bit about Lucas's vocabulary development.

Formative assessment (sometimes called informal assessment or assessment for learning) is a plan to gather day-to-day information about learners, what they are learning, and what they need to learn. The Council of Chief State School Officers defines formative assessment as "a process used by teachers and students during instruction that provides feedback to adjust ongoing teaching and learning to improve students' achievement of intended outcomes" (2008, 3).

Robert Stakes, an education evaluation specialist, is credited with saying, "When the cook tastes the soup, that's formative; when the guests taste the soup, that's summative." To extend the metaphor, formative assessment tells us if the soup needs more salt or if we need to thicken the broth before we serve it in its final form, and the guests determine whether we have mastered the art of soup making.

A classroom that infuses formative assessment often becomes a student-centered classroom (Garrison 2009). When teachers intentionally use formative assessment, they are more attuned to student learning. That is, they are always looking for clues to what students know or don't know and are responding to those clues. In a student-centered classroom, students feel more at ease in taking academic risks. Making learning a shared responsibility means students begin to help each other and develop self-reliance.

In urging teachers to focus more on assessment *for* learning rather than assessment *of* learning, Siobhan Leahy, Christine Lyon, Marnie Thompson, and Dylan Wiliam (2005) write, "In a classroom that uses assessment to support learning, the divide between instruction and assessment blurs. Everything students do—such as conversing in groups, completing seatwork, answering and asking questions, working on projects, handing in homework assignments, even sitting silently and looking confused—is a potential source of information about how much they understand" (19). In their research, the authors have determined that five assessment strategies are effective for teachers at all grade levels:

1. Clarifying and sharing learning intentions and criteria for success,
2. Engineering effective classroom discussions, questions, and learning tasks,
3. Providing feedback that moves learners forward,
4. Activating students as the owners of their own learning, and
5. Activating students as instructional resources for one another. (20)

As mentioned before, we believe this more generalized research about assessment can help us improve assessment of vocabulary development. In working with our students, we have found that the type of learning environment generated by formative assessment is vital for high-poverty students who are typically passive recipients of information rather than active participants in learning. As we teach vocabulary, we want to instill a purpose for learning. We consistently discuss the benefits of college and the possibilities of the future, trying to encourage a sense of urgency about vocabulary development. We then look for evidence that students understand why it is important to use expressive words and phrases in their daily work. When we involve them in academic discussions about particular words, they learn word connections, nuances of word relationships, shades of meaning, and how to apply words in context. When we provide immediate feedback and correct misconceptions throughout each vocabulary cycle, we are teaching as well as assessing. By using a variety of authentic, formative assessments, we create a culture where every person is available to help every other person learn. And when students know they possess the power to learn, they have ownership of their education.

Methods of Formative Assessment

Throughout the book, we have discussed many ways we use research-based formative assessment to determine student understanding of vocabulary. Here we gather these strategies into one place and discuss their optimal timing and value. In Figure 8.2, we outline the types of formative assessments we use. In the following sections, we discuss each of the strategies in detail.

Assessment Strategy	Used When Assessing . . .	To Analyze . . .
Thumbs Up/ Thumbs Down	Introduction of Words	Understanding of word meanings and words in context
	Synonyms and Antonyms	Understanding of word relationships
Observation	Synonyms and Antonyms	Use of reference materials
	Counting Dude/Bragging Dude	Applying words in context in a sentence of seven words or more
	Scramble	Applying word relationships
	Vocabulary Rap	Knowledge of word relationships
	Line It Up	Remembering word meanings
	Crystal Ball Words	Analyzing meanings of word parts
	Word Charades	Creating a new way to think about the meaning of a word (higher-order thinking)
	Chain Link	Creating a new way to think about word relationships (higher-order thinking)
	Review Games	Understanding and applying word meanings and relationships
Analyzing Student Work	Vocabulary Journals	Understanding and applying word meanings and relationships
	Vocabulary Rings	Understanding and applying word meanings and relationships
	Word Illustrations	Creating a new way to think about the meaning of a word (higher-order thinking)
	Word Colors	Creating a new way to think about the meaning of a word (higher-order thinking)
	PowerPoint Portrayals	Creating a new way to think about the meaning of a word (higher-order thinking); use of technology
	Peer Assessment of PowerPoint Portrayal	Evaluating use of vocabulary, use of technology, and speaking and listening
Teacher Questioning	All activities	Remembering, understanding, applying, and analyzing word meanings and relationships
	Use of Whiteboards	Remembering, understanding, applying, and analyzing word meanings and relationships
Student-Generated Questions	Board Games	Remembering, understanding, applying, and analyzing word meanings and relationships
	Review Games	Remembering, understanding, applying, and analyzing word meanings and relationships
	Celebrations	Remembering, understanding, applying, and analyzing word meanings and relationships

Figure 8.2 *Formative Assessment Chart for vocabulary instruction*

Thumbs Up, Thumbs Down

We often use overt measures of formative assessment, such as Thumbs Up, Thumbs Down, to gauge understanding during vocabulary lessons and promote active learning. Thumbs Up, Thumbs Down is an easy way to take the pulse of a group while also looking for individual responses.

While introducing words on the pocket chart or asking students to predict the exact word that would fit into the blank in a cloze sentence, we encourage students to put their thumbs up if they agree with a classmate's answer, put their thumbs down if they do not agree, and put their thumbs sideways if they are not sure. This method ensures that all students are engaged, and we can quickly see who understands. Using the thumbs response also promotes classroom community and academic risk taking because no one is allowed to be passive and everyone will probably be right or wrong at some point. In Thumbs Up, Thumbs Down, we not only rely on the responses students indicate with their fingers, but we also pair student responses with observation of facial clues and body language. If students are shy about sharing or are looking to others for guidance before they respond, we could ask them to hold their thumbs close to their bodies so no one else but the teacher can see. But we have rarely resorted to this secretive process because in a learning community that feels academically safe, students are usually not afraid to be wrong (see Figure 8.3).

Figure 8.3 *Leslie's students indicate Thumbs Up, Thumbs Down.*

Observation

Margot and her third graders are gathered around the pocket chart in a corner of the classroom. They have reached the end of a first-day vocabulary lesson where Margot has introduced three words for a two-week vocabulary cycle. Margot needs to gauge student understanding of the words in this particular lesson, so she guides students to discuss their knowledge as part of a quick assessment:

Margot: Can you tell me something new you have learned about a word today?

James:	I learned that *distinguished* has two meanings.
Sara:	I learned that *monitor* means to watch or keep track of something. I didn't know that word before.
Margot:	We have also talked about similes this week. Can I challenge anyone to think of a simile using a vocabulary word?
Brianna:	Writing is like a voyage. It takes a long time to do all the stages!

Margot observes that James and Sara are on their way to understanding the words *distinguished* and *monitor* and that Brianna is confident in her knowledge of similes. Using observation as formative assessment, Margot decides that she can move on to the next day's lesson.

In every vocabulary lesson or activity, we carefully "kid-watch" (Goodman 1978) for student reactions and responses. We observe facial expressions to see if students display excitement or bewilderment. We observe body language—is the student actively leaning forward and making eye contact with others, or is he hanging back, which may mean he lacks the word confidence to participate? We observe who is in the middle of an activity and who is on the periphery. When students are working in small groups to find synonyms and antonyms, create word charades, or play a board game, we circulate and listen to their conversations. We note which students seem accurate and confident with the words and which students seem hesitant. As students play *Jeopardy!* or Line It Up or participate in Vocabulary Parties, we listen for their use of vocabulary and analyze their thinking about the words. Sometimes we jot down notes to help us remember. Sometimes we store the information in the back of our minds for later. In any case, we encourage and clarify student vocabulary learning and application as the situation requires.

For example, during Counting Dude, Bragging Dude, Leslie walks around the room listening to students' 7-Up sentences. Alexis is wearing the word *curiosity*. When Alexis says, "I am curiosity to meet you and learn more about you," she is using the word incorrectly but she does demonstrate an understanding of the root word. Leslie chooses not to correct Alexis because the goal at this point of the vocabulary cycle is for Alexis to take a risk using new words. Instead, Leslie decides to incorporate a quick mini-lesson into her next day's activities so she can share with the whole class how a suffix can change the part of speech. The class then practices sentences using the adjective *curious* and the noun *curiosity*.

Observation can tell us a lot about our students' learning if we take the time to pay attention. As Yogi Berra said, "You can observe a lot just by watching."

Analyzing Student Work

In strategic vocabulary instruction, student work is generated almost on a daily basis. We review and analyze these work samples for evidence of thinking, learning, and misconceptions.

For example, students complete a vocabulary journal entry for every word that is introduced. On the graphic organizer provided in their journal folders, they list the word, a kid-friendly definition, and synonyms/examples and antonyms/non-examples. They also sketch the concept and write a sentence using at least seven words. We quickly review their entries to make sure the words are spelled correctly and the synonyms and antonyms are captured accurately. We then analyze the sketch to see if students understand the concept we have discussed as a class and the seven-word sentence to see how the student has applied the word. We do not grade the journals, but because students use their journals as a resource throughout the year (and we have delightedly caught kids using their journals from previous years in class during vocabulary lessons) we want to make sure their entries are accurate. Perhaps Jordan has written a sentence with only five words, so we ask him to write a more expanded sentence that captures the definition of a word the way we have introduced it in class. Maybe De'Jayne has drawn a sketch of the word *distribution* that doesn't capture the word's meaning. In that case, we ask her to explain her reasoning. If necessary, we then ask her to draw a new sketch that more fully addresses the concept.

Other student samples include word illustrations and artwork, creative presentations, graphic organizers, writing, or multimedia projects. As students work together in small groups, we can analyze any work they produce for evidence of learning and understanding.

Teacher Questioning

Another overt way we use formative assessment to check for understanding is through questioning. Peter Afflerbach (2012) describes the typical assessment questioning technique in most classrooms as the "initiate-respond-evaluate (IRE) discourse form." In the IRE form in many lessons, the teacher asks a student a question requiring a simple answer, and the student supplies the answer. The teacher then tells the student if the answer was correct or incorrect. Afflerbach gives this example that is focused on vocabulary:

> *Initiate (Teacher):* What is a compass rose?
> *Respond (Student):* It's the part of a map that shows directions.
> *Evaluate (Teacher):* Yes, that's correct. (53)

Although we have all resorted to such simplistic questioning at one time or another, we try to ask vocabulary questions that require students to analyze and apply information rather than give one-word rote answers or simple definitions. We provide sufficient wait time for student responses and encourage them if they need help. By increasing the amount of wait time after asking a question, Mary Budd Rowe (1986) found that teachers can encourage more student talk and more student-to-student interactions. We want to make sure our students have time to think about vocabulary use when they are first learning words. We listen for complete and accurate answers and affirm and expand thinking. For example, the simple IRE question mentioned previously could be transformed into vocabulary study like this:

Initiate (Teacher):	How might an explorer use a compass rose? (*waits for an answer*)
Respond (Student):	The explorer would see a compass rose on the map and know what direction is north.
Evaluate (Teacher):	Yes, a compass rose shows directions on a map.

In this IRE example, the teacher gives appropriate wait time so that students can think of a deeper response, and the student is taught to provide an answer that requires application. The teacher then responds in a way that elaborates on student understanding.

As Afflerbach (2012) points out, the IRE format is teacher directed and establishes "a teacher monopoly on assessment" (61). Although we don't think the one-word-answer format constitutes good teaching and we don't believe that the IRE question format is the only one we should use, we do recognize that students need teacher guidance and affirmation as models for thinking about vocabulary during academic discussions. We use the more sophisticated IRE format often in our vocabulary lessons as a scaffold to more elaborated forms of collaborative and student-generated conversations about words and concepts.

When we question, we also find ways for all students to answer rather than one at a time. In many of our vocabulary lessons and games, each student has an individual whiteboard, a marker, and an eraser. When we ask a question, each student writes the answer on his or her whiteboard and holds it up in the air. We can easily see who has correct or incorrect answers. This helps us know when and what we need to reteach.

Student-Generated Questions

As the year progresses and students become more word confident, we encourage a scaffolded approach in which students begin to ask their own questions of themselves and peers. We intentionally plan vocabulary activities where student questioning is part of the lesson. Students write the questions for class games and ask each other questions in whole- and small-group activities. When students ask and answer questions, we listen for vocabulary knowledge in what they say. By listening carefully, we know to teach or reteach as necessary.

For example, Leslie was teaching her students the difference between writing "thin" (literal level or memorization) questions and "thick" (thoughtful and meaningful) questions. After the lesson, she asked her students to write some of the more expansive vocabulary questions to use in the next day's vocabulary celebration. For the word *passage*, T.J. wrote, "Fill in the blank: You are lost in the woods and looking for safe_____." We considered this to be a good example of a "thick" question for several reasons. As far as we know, T.J. has not been to a forest. He had learned the meaning of *passage* in a social studies context, and Leslie had recently read aloud a chapter in *The Lightning Thief* (Riordan 2005), where Percy Jackson is lost in the woods and must find his way out. T.J. not only connected his question both to the real world and to a text, but also wrote a question with an interesting turn of phrase. His classmates would have to apply their knowledge of vocabulary to answer it.

In contrast, Sara's contribution, "What is a synonym for *passage*?" was a thin question containing basic information she took straight from her journal. Leslie recognized that Sara needed more instruction to help her expand her thinking.

We have found that our students are only able to ask thick questions about vocabulary words if they truly understand the word they are writing about, and so the questions they generate become a form of assessment about their vocabulary learning. When Olivia asks, "Can you tell about a time when you had to make a *sacrifice*?" her classmates cannot answer the question accurately unless they know what the word *sacrifice* means. In addition, we can see that Olivia understands the word by the way she phrased her question.

Such exchanges also help us assess our teaching. If our students are consistently asking "thin" vocabulary questions, then we may not be modeling well enough or giving them enough time for the active practice they need to learn the words in a deeper way.

Summative Vocabulary Assessment

When we complete a vocabulary cycle, we give a teacher-developed test as a summative assessment. We intentionally design our summative assessments to look like the vocabulary sections on many standardized tests. We want students to learn to negotiate the terminology and format of common tests, recognizing them as another literary genre (see *Test Talk: Integrating Test Preparation into Reading Workshop* [Greene and Melton 2007] and *Put Thinking to the Test* [Conrad et al. 2008]).

Mirroring the cloze activity we use to introduce words at the beginning of the vocabulary cycle (see Chapter 3), we close this vocabulary cycle with an assessment consisting of sentences that contain blanks to be filled in with appropriate vocabulary words in a passage. We intentionally assess with this format because it correlates with how students will see words in text passages and on many standardized tests. Students have to be able to see the big picture and use context clues in order to fill in the blanks correctly. On the second page of the assessment we include multiple-choice items. These items usually consist of a phrase with a bolded word and four synonym choices for the word (often including words from past units as choices). You can see an example of Leslie's teacher-created test in Figure 8.4. The passage is in the form of a letter to a student teacher.

VOCABULARY WEEK #4

Name: _____   Date: _____

Word Bank:
scarcity   navigate   colonization   conflict   prejudice   economy

Dear Mrs. Hammer,

How are you? I wanted to let you know what we have been doing in school this week. In social studies class we are learning how explorers from Spain, France, and England came to America (the New World) to find riches and a route to Asia. The riches and resources that were found in the New World were taken back to their sponsor country to improve their _____. Many of these explorers started settlements. These explorations and settlements led to the _____ of the New World. I am excited because we are going to start learning about the first colonies next week!

Many of the explorers plotted a course and used a compass to _____ their way to the New World. After months on the ships, they often arrived to the New World with a _____ of resources. Often _____ was caused between the Europeans and Native Americans when the Europeans took the resources the Native Americans needed to survive. Europeans were unfamiliar with the Native Americans and had a _____ toward them. Often they were treated as unintelligent, heartless savages.

I hope you have a wonderful weekend. I look forward to seeing you on Tuesday!

Sincerely,

Your favorite student

Bonus question: Using your context clues, what does the word *savages* mean in the passage?

_____

_____

_____

_____

Figure 8.4 *Leslie's teacher-created vocabulary test*

We also teach students how to approach an assessment and apply test-taking skills to find clues to the correct words, such as using context clues and the process of elimination. Practice builds their confidence before they have to take a test that carries a grade or a standardized score. We also debrief after they take practice exams so they can verbalize their thinking and we can reinforce the appropriate use of the words and correct any misconceptions. Teaching students how to take a vocabulary assessment is not teaching to the test. We believe our students need low-risk opportunities to get used to the type of high-stakes assessment they will take to determine their futures (see Figure 8.5).

Figure 8.5 *Shaylee works on a summative vocabulary assessment.*

Thinking Through Summative Assessment in Third Grade

Let's see how this process plays out in Margot's third-grade class. Using a practice test that she has written and projected onto the whiteboard, she features the words *transit*, *frontier*, *construction*, *technology*, and *elegant*. The students each have a copy of the practice assessment in front of them. Margot leads a class discussion to help her students "think through" methods of approaching these tests (Conrad et al. 2008).

She deliberately uses the word *test* so that students will not get nervous when they hear the word in the future. Our students have a tendency to freeze when first presented with any type of formal assessment. Although they may know the content, they often become so anxious when they see a test that they forget what they are supposed to do. We have to provide positive experiences so they will believe in their abilities and transfer the skills they've shown us in the classroom.

Margot continues, "First, I want to remind you that I'm not going to get mad if you write notes on your test paper to help you remember. I'm going to say, 'Wow! Daneasha is really thinking and trying to get these words right!'"

Daneasha smiles and wiggles a bit, apparently pleased at the attention from her teacher.

Margot continues, "Okay, let's talk about how to take the test. Remember I have told you there are some good rules to follow. One of the rules is not to guess without evidence.

You need to use all your resources and clues to figure out the answer. Your resources are your vocabulary notebooks, charts in the room, the pocket chart with the sentences on it, and anything else that can help you." There is a rustle in the room as students get out their vocabulary journals. Although Margot does not allow the students to use the journals when taking the assessment, she wants them to remember to consult the journal as a resource when thinking about the words. "Now let's talk about the clues you might find."

Margot demonstrates how to think about each word, the appropriate part of speech, a kid-friendly definition, and synonyms. While she makes notes, students do the same thing on their papers: *Transit* is a noun (a thing) that often goes with the word *system*, and means the way goods or people are carried.

"Now I want you to look at the word *construction*. What small word do you see inside of the word *construction*?"

Alexis raises her hand. "I know. It's *construct*."

"Yes, that is correct." Margot draws a box around the part of the word that contains *construct* and directs students to draw a similar box on their papers. "What does the word *construct* mean?" she asks. "Maria?"

"It means to build," answers Maria.

"Right! So that's an example of a clue that can help you figure out the meaning of a word and where they make sense in a sentence. *Construction* is a noun (a thing) that means something that has been built."

Margot then reads the passage aloud and models how she would underline key terms to help her build meaning. Next, she moves away from the computer and steps up to the whiteboard. "Now I am going to show you how I think about a test like this. Please just listen and don't call out any answers."

She then proceeds to do a verbal think-aloud so that students can experience how an expert test taker goes about approaching a vocabulary test. Think-alouds are often used by effective literacy teachers to model their own thinking (Davey 1983). In a think-aloud, the teacher talks about what she is thinking as she approaches a task such as using comprehension strategies or problems with word recognition. Today Margot talks loud enough so that the students can hear her yet in a softer tone than usual so students will know she is thinking. She also points her index finger at her forehead occasionally while she talks to indicate that she is thinking.

"Well, first, I can infer that the passage is about the past because it starts by saying, 'many years ago.'

"Now I'm looking at the first blank. I am looking for the best word out of my choices to go into this sentence. I don't really see enough clues in the first sentence, so I'll go on to the next one. . . ." Her voice drifts off.

At his desk, Matthew whispers, "Come on, Miss Holmes. You can do it!"

Margot resumes. "Oh! I see a lot of clues here to tell me what might go in the first blank. The word *settled* might be a clue because I know it means people made their homes there. Maybe it's a clue that means there weren't very many people living there. I'm thinking it might be *frontier* since a frontier is a noun that is a place and it means natural, unsettled land." She uses the stylus to write the word *frontier* in the blank in the sentence on the whiteboard.

"In this blank, I am thinking the word might be an adjective because it is in front of a noun. The women made necklaces and bracelets that were colorful. The word might mean that the necklaces and bracelets were pretty. The word *elegant* might fit since it is an adjective and a synonym for pretty." She writes *elegant* in the blank.

"In the next sentence, I'm not sure what a telegraph is. But do I really need to know specifically what a telegraph is? No, I don't. I just need to know it was something that helped people communicate better. I'm looking to see what word it might be. Maybe *technology*, since that has to do with communication." She adds the word *technology* to the third blank.

"In the fourth blank, my clues are 'new houses and buildings' and the word *built*. I know the word *construction* has the little word *construct* in it, which means to build." She writes in *construction*.

"For the last one, I have a really good clue. The word *system* comes after the blank, and there are clues that tell me it is used to get to and from places. I know that *transit* goes with *system* and means a way to move things. I remember that we talked about the fact that the words *transit* and *system* are 'best friend' words and they go together like peanut butter and jelly. All right, I am almost finished." She writes *transit* in the last blank.

"Okay, now I am finished. Do I flip my paper over and do the other side? No, I do not. I reread it to make sure I have made the right choices."

Margot steps away from the whiteboard and back to the laptop. She says to the students, "Reread the passage with me. Follow the pencil and let's read together." She uses the curser (that looks like a little pencil) to draw attention to each word as they read each sentence aloud with the word in the blank. They decide that each sentence has the correct word.

"But I want you to think about this a little bit more," Margot continues. "When I'm taking a vocabulary test, what happens if I'm left with two choices and I can't decide which one is right?" She uses the eraser feature to remove the words *elegant* and *technology* from the blanks. Then she switches the words, so that the phrases now read "technology necklaces and bracelets" and "a elegant system."

Micah exclaims, "Hey, that sounds like a pretty system!"

Margot chuckles with the rest of the class, and then jots the word *noun* above each of the words *necklace* and *bracelet*.

"This is the way I might think about it. What part of speech is the word *technology*, Kayla?" Margot asks.

"It's a noun," replies Kayla.

"Right. Do nouns usually describe nouns?" continues Margot.

Heads shake around the room. "No, adjectives usually describe nouns. I would automatically rule out the word *technology* because it doesn't really fit into that place in the sentence.

"Now, let's look at the other one. There is a small but powerful clue to tell you that the word *elegant* is wrong in this blank. It's a dead giveaway! You have to look at the little word

Dear Mr. Cooper,

Did you know I am a Native American? We hunt buffalo and we grow crops. We are a _____ tribe, we follow our food.

We _____ on the men to hunt for the food. We _____ with other tribes for their rabbit skins. Our _____ is dancing to honor the spirits of the animals that gave their lives for us.

Sometimes we _____ south for the warmer weather in search of food. We then have to _____ to a new environment.

We are having a good time and we play lots of games.

See you at school.

Sincerely,

Tayaunna

Figure 8.6 *Tayaunna's self-created vocabulary quiz*

in front of the blank. Is it *a* or is it *an*? Remember, if it is *a*, the word has to start with a consonant. If it is *an*, it has to start with a vowel. So many of you did this last week. You can't just go in and add *a* in front of a blank on a test. Remember that for the rest of your lives.

"Tomorrow, you will get another practice assessment. I'll guide you through the beginning, and then you will complete it on your own. Friday you will take a test independently. Next week, I'm going to ask you to create a test with a partner, and then lead us through how you might teach your classmates to take your test."

On another day, Margot leads her students through similar techniques to approach the multiple-choice side of the assessment.

We often ask students to create vocabulary tests as a way for them to think deeply about appropriate ways to apply the words. We then choose a student-created test and give it to the class as a practice quiz. Figure 8.6 shows Tayaunna's vocabulary quiz.

Analyzing Summative Assessments

We grade our tests and quizzes so we can report results to parents and administrators. More important than grades, however, is the assessment analysis that we do throughout the year. After our students take an assessment, we evaluate any errors and maintain a record of how our students are progressing. Because of the consistency of our routine, students are adding to their vocabulary knowledge from week to week. If one or two students do not do well on an assessment, it usually indicates that they have an issue with learning the words or word relationships. If most of the students do poorly, it probably means we are doing something in the classroom that hasn't resonated with the kids, or we are not doing something we should. As Leslie wryly says, "If several of my kids don't perform well on a vocabulary test, I really have to look at my instruction. If I'm honest with myself, I know it's probably because I didn't think enough about the needs of the kids or take the time to engage them in active learning. The kids let me know it every time."

The nature of the vocabulary test we have developed lets us see what students can do with the vocabulary words. When we review how students have placed the words in the blanks in the passage, we analyze how well students understand and can apply words in context. When we review the part of the assessment with highlighted words where students must choose the correct synonym, we analyze students' understanding of word relationships. Because so many of our vocabulary words in the intermediate grades are subject-specific words, we can also often tell if individual students understand key social studies or science concepts. For example, when Keesha always does well on social studies words but makes errors when the words focus on science, we understand more about Keesha's academic needs. When DeWayne is successful in choosing the correct synonyms on the multiple-choice section, but has trouble with the passage with the cloze sentences, we know he understands the vocabulary but is having a problem with comprehension. When Samuel gets some words right and some wrong on the cloze passage, especially for those words that are close in meaning, it could well mean that he is not using strategies to check for the best answer. When Hayley puts the word *remarkable* into a blank that has the word *an* in front of it, we know she either is not looking for details in context clues or does not understand that *an* only comes before a word that begins with a vowel—both important test-taking strategies. Our summative assessments not only produce a grade, they also tell us about our students.

Charting Vocabulary Progress

Using a vocabulary rubric we developed, we can analyze our students' progress for each unit (see Figure 8.7). Throughout the unit, we also review evidence we have collected through formative and summative assessments. Then we complete the rubric to help us plan instruction for the next unit.

We also use a Vocabulary Progress Form to keep track of our students' vocabulary development (see Figure 8.8 and Appendix H). We have used this form in various ways. Sometimes we write groups of students' names in the boxes according to their level of mastery

Name: _____   **Date:** _____

Demonstrates . . .	Mastered	Almost Mastered	Not Yet Mastered
Appropriate use of vocabulary in sentences of seven or more words	Student can use vocabulary appropriately in sentences of seven or more words.	Student can use vocabulary appropriately in a sentence of fewer than seven words.	Student cannot consistently use vocabulary appropriately in sentences.
Ability to determine meanings of vocabulary words in context	Student can determine meanings of vocabulary words in context in a sentence or passage of text.	Student can identify meanings of vocabulary words.	Student cannot identify or determine meanings of vocabulary words.
Ability to determine word relationships (such as synonyms/ examples, antonyms/ non-examples)	Student can identify and correctly use synonyms/examples and antonyms/non-examples for vocabulary words.	Student can identify only synonym/ examples or antonyms/non-examples for vocabulary words.	Student cannot identify synonyms/examples or antonyms/non-examples for vocabulary words.
Ability to determine nuances in word meaning (for example, shades of meaning such as _happy_, _cheerful_, _overjoyed_)	Student can determine and apply shades of meaning of adjectives and verbs.	Student can determine but not apply shades of meanings of adjectives and/or verbs.	Student cannot determine shades of word meaning.
Ability to interpret literal or nonliteral or figurative language (such as similes, metaphors, idioms)	Student can interpret the meaning of literal, nonliteral, or figurative language in a sentence or passage.	Student can identify the meaning of literal, nonliteral, or figurative language.	Student cannot identify the meaning of literal, nonliteral, or figurative language.
Understanding of affixes and roots as clues to the meaning of a word	Student can use the meanings of both affixes and roots to determine the meaning of a word.	Student can use the meanings of affixes or roots to determine the meaning of a word.	Student cannot use the meanings of affixes or roots to determine the meaning of a word.

Figure 8.7 _Vocabulary Unit with related assessments_

Understanding use of reference materials	Student can use appropriate reference materials independently.	Student can use appropriate reference materials with assistance.	Student is not able to use reference materials.
Higher-order thinking about vocabulary	Student can engage successfully in learning experiences that demonstrate higher-order thinking about vocabulary.	Student engages in learning experiences that show limited evidence of higher-order thinking about vocabulary.	Student only displays literal thinking in vocabulary learning experiences.
Application of vocabulary words outside of vocabulary instruction (in conversation or in other student work)	Student uses vocabulary appropriately and extensively outside of vocabulary instruction or assessment experiences.	Student uses vocabulary appropriately outside of vocabulary instruction or assessment experiences in a limited way.	Student does not use vocabulary except during vocabulary instruction or assessment experiences.

Figure 8.7 *continued*

during a vocabulary cycle. Other times we use a page for each student and keep a notebook of all of their progress. We find the more we use the form, the less we need it as we become highly aware of each student's agility with vocabulary concepts.

Assessment: A Window into Vocabulary Development

Ongoing assessment helps us gauge language our students already know, take a look at their understanding of new words, and evaluate their ability to apply vocabulary before we move to the next lesson. Summative assessment helps us to evaluate the vocabulary gains our students have made and gives us a way to report that progress outside our classrooms.

There is no doubt about it—teaching vocabulary in the way we have described in this book takes time and effort. It would be hard to justify the emphasis we give vocabulary in our classrooms if we didn't see the results every day. We believe that our students' assessment results tell the story of their learning and send a strong message that strategic vocabulary instruction is vital to the academic achievement of at-risk students.

Vocabulary Progress Form

Directions: Record student names in the appropriate boxes for each vocabulary cycle or use one form per student to record anecdotal notes.

Vocabulary Cycle: Date:

Demonstrates . . .	Mastered	Almost Mastered	Not Yet Mastered
Appropriate use of vocabulary word in sentences of seven or more words			
Ability to determine meanings of vocabulary words in context			
Ability to determine word relationships (synonyms/ examples, antonyms/non-examples)			
Ability to determine nuances in word meaning (shades of meaning)			
Ability to interpret literal or nonliteral or figurative language (similes, metaphors, idioms)			
Understanding of affixes and roots as clues to meaning of a word			
Understanding of use of reference materials			
Higher-order thinking about vocabulary			
Application of vocabulary words outside of vocabulary instruction (in conversation or in other student work)			

Figure 8.8 *Vocabulary Progress Form*

Epilogue: End of the Year

As we finish this book, it is a glorious spring and we are close to concluding another school year. A pile of paperwork awaits our attention, and the to-do list just gets longer. We glance a bit wistfully out the window at the bright sunshine as we take a minute to get organized before we walk down the hall to attend one of our last faculty meetings. Suddenly, there is a knock at the door. Maddy, one of our former students who is about to finish her first year in middle school, pokes her head into Leslie's classroom.

"Hi, Ms. Montgomery. I just came to tell you that you were wrong," Maddy says with a droll smile on her face.

"Maddy! I'm so glad to see you!" exclaims Leslie, giving Maddy a big hug. "But, oh my! Why was I wrong?"

"You told us all the time that middle school was going to be difficult and we had to get ready. But you were wrong. It's not that hard," Maddie announces confidently, handing Leslie a certificate that shows she made the honor roll for most of her sixth-grade year. Then Maddy insists on going to the faculty meeting with Leslie and telling all the teachers about her success.

Although home and community challenges have not changed for our former students, we have heard from many like Maddy that their preparation at Atkinson helped them overcome barriers that might have kept them from learning. Parents and middle school teachers have also shared stories of our students' successes, such as being admitted to the advanced program or selective middle schools in our "school choice" district. Some of our former students have won academic awards or have been asked to represent their middle schools at prestigious events.

Although Maddy believes that middle school is easy, we feel sure that part of the reason is a sense of confidence our students carry with them that grows from their experiences in elementary school. When Stacie calls to tell us about an invitation to study in our nation's capital and breezes through words such as *ambassador*, *delegate*, and *represent*, we know she still remembers vocabulary she learned with us. When Demetria emails to thank us because she has an exceptionally high test score in reading, or Dante drops by just to tell us he is doing well, our hearts soar in celebration with them. Their stories, along with rising test scores, remind us that our word nerds are truly learning and loving vocabulary.

As we worked on this project, we learned what it takes to increase vocabulary development among children who are growing up under highly challenging circumstances and come to school with a limited vocabulary base. Knowledge, commitment, time, energy, and organization are all necessary to implement a strategic vocabulary plan that will serve them well. In short, teachers must:

- Establish an environment where vocabulary development can thrive and students are comfortable taking academic risks.
- Develop a teaching routine where vocabulary development is front and center.
- Model the behaviors we want to see in the classroom so students can learn successfully.
- Plan instruction that keeps students engaged in active learning and progressing toward word command.
- Use a variety of assessments that help us evaluate their progress before, during, and after that instruction.
- Celebrate vocabulary learning!

Implementing such a plan is not for the faint of heart. It takes dedication and a lot of hard work. Yet it is indisputable if we wish to ensure that our students are engrossed in the type of vocabulary instruction they need for high achievement.

Vocabulary Power!

When asked to share our vocabulary plan at conferences, professional development sessions, and other venues, we have encountered many teachers who are excited to create a strategic vocabulary plan in their own classrooms. In Chapter 3 we shared Ashlee Kemper's efforts to take the plan back to her second-grade classroom where almost half her students are English language learners. In visits to her classroom, we have seen the power of strategic vocabulary instruction with new English speakers. Ashlee is following all the steps of our strategic vocabulary plan, but has made adaptions for the needs of her particular second-grade class.

One change is that she introduces vocabulary words in both English and Spanish for the entire class. Another adaption is using "word castles" instead of "word entourages" for her young primary students. At a signal from Ashlee, students travel to word castles to meet with the "king" or "queen," who are wearing the vocabulary word. The students wearing the synonym and antonym lanyards are the "prince" or "princess" of that particular castle. A third adaption is that when Ashlee's students hear a word they have been taught during vocabulary instruction, they raise their hand with their first two fingers like a "V" (an idea from a teacher on Ashlee's team). Asked about this, the students smile broadly and tell us "it means V Power!" Of course, the *V* stands for Vocabulary. It is a matter of course to hear Ashlee's students using new vocabulary words in all content areas. That is V Power, indeed.

Sharon is a teacher who is implementing a strategic vocabulary plan with her fourth-grade students in a neighboring school district. Although more reserved than the students at Atkinson, Sharon's kids enjoy the vocabulary experiences just as much. More important, Sharon has also seen an increase in their classroom academic achievement.

Melissa, a teacher in a school in a more affluent community outside Louisville, has also adopted strategic vocabulary instruction with her third graders. In addition to following our plan, she has been experimenting with ways that technology can support different parts of vocabulary instruction.

Several of our colleagues who teach kindergarten and first grade have adapted the plan to meet the needs of their students. They teach fewer words at a time and rely on more pictures. Although they use our graphic organizers with their students, they introduce the parts of the organizer in smaller pieces with a lot of teacher support until their students are able to work more independently.

We know of several Kentucky Reading Project participants who took the information back to their schools, and shared it during school-based professional development. Their schools are now implementing strategic vocabulary instruction from kindergarten through grade five, with positive results.

We are always glad to hear how other teachers are adapting our strategic vocabulary plan because we get to learn new ideas and celebrate their successes. We welcome other strategies from readers, who can help us continue to motivate and teach our students well.

One way we are focusing our professional development is to ensure that we are addressing all of the Common Core State Standards. We know there is a new focus on vocabulary as part of the Common Core, but we also know that application of the vocabulary standards will need to be integrated throughout English language arts and other content areas. We are reading about, thinking about, and discussing ways to continue the strategic vocabulary instruction plan that has been so successful with our students, but also looking at ways to integrate vocabulary for richer instruction and learning across the curriculum.

Introduce, Initiate, Inaugurate!

If you are interested in pursuing a strategic vocabulary plan, consider following these steps to get started. First, discuss it with your colleagues. Find out if any of your colleagues would like to join you on this journey. We know many teachers who have implemented this plan alone in their own classrooms, but it is certainly easier when you are part of a team. With other teachers, you can share resources, collaboratively design lessons and assessments, and analyze student progress together. Consider creating a schoolwide plan where students learn vocabulary across the school day. A unified effort will go a long way toward helping students develop the vocabulary acquisition and knowledge they need to become successful in school and in life.

Second, initiate the plan by putting it down on paper. Determine how you will assess your students for vocabulary knowledge and how vocabulary instruction will become part of your daily schedule. What learning experiences are appropriate for your students? How will you need to set up or rearrange your classroom? What resources will you need, and where will you get them? What do you still need to learn about vocabulary teaching? A glance through the references at the end of this book will give you several ideas. In particular, we recommend the following resources to help you get started:

- *The Next Step in Vocabulary Instruction: Practical Strategies and Engaging Activities That Help All Learners Build Vocabulary and Deepen Comprehension*, by Karen Bromley (Scholastic, 2012). This book is an excellent teaching resource for grades one through eight and contains a multitude of instructional ideas to add to a strategic vocabulary routine.
- *Words, Words, Words: Teaching Vocabulary in Grades 4–12*, by Janet Allen (Stenhouse, 1999). Although this book was written with older students in mind, most of the information and strategies are applicable for younger students as well. A brief, to-the-point resource.
- *Essential Readings on Vocabulary Instruction*, compiled and introduced by Michael Graves (International Reading Association, 2009). This book is an edited volume with each chapter focused on a different aspect of vocabulary instruction. The authors of the chapters are experts in the field and include practical ideas and resources for vocabulary instruction.
- *Teaching Vocabulary in All Classrooms*, 4th ed., by Camille Blachowicz and Peter J. Fisher (Allyn & Bacon, 2009). A rich resource of strategies and ideas for enhancing K–12 vocabulary instruction.
- *The Vocabulary-Enriched Classroom: Practices for Improving Reading Performance of All Students in Grades 3 and Up*, edited by Cathy Collins Block and John N. Mangieri (Scholastic, 2006). This book is an edited work, with varied authors writing each chapter in a teacher-friendly, practical way. Contains teaching and assessment ideas.
- *Bringing Words to Life: Robust Vocabulary Instruction*, by Isabel Beck, Margaret McKeown, and Linda Kucan (Guilford Press, 2002). The ultimate resource on vocabulary teaching and learning, this book is based on the authors' research.

- A subscription to the International Reading Association will bring with it access to *The Reading Teacher*, an excellent teacher-oriented journal with research-based ideas about different aspects of literacy, including vocabulary. See www.reading.org.

Finally, inaugurate the plan. As the NIKE ad says, "Just do it." Set up your classroom, plan your first vocabulary cycle, and begin. Establish a routine your students can count on. Remember that, as with anything, it will get easier as you become more experienced.

The Last Word

A recent newspaper headline recounts the story of Dawn Loggins, a high school senior in North Carolina, who returned from an academic summer program to find that her family had moved away. According to CNN News, Dawn grew up under conditions most of us would consider appalling—hunger, no running water, no electricity, and no clean clothing. Her parents were drug abusers and jobless. When they abandoned Dawn, she got a job as a janitor at her high school and slept on a friend's sofa. With support from the adults at her school and community and her own indomitable will to succeed, she was accepted to Harvard University on a full scholarship.

Her story reminds us of the elementary students all around us who are growing up in challenging circumstances yet have high potential. Cultivating and celebrating their intelligence, wit, enthusiasm, and resilience is part of our job as teachers. Vocabulary knowledge is a crucial part of the skill set they need to succeed, and we must give them the tools. Their future depends on us.

Appendix A

Vocabulary Planner

Word	Kid-Friendly Definition	Sentence	Synonym(s) or Examples	Antonym(s) or Non-Examples	Picture	Idioms and/or Other Meanings

Extra Word Definitions

Created by Maria Carrico

Word Nerds: Teaching All Students to Learn and Love Vocabulary by Brenda J. Overturf, Leslie H. Montgomery, and Margot Holmes Smith. ©2013. Stenhouse Publishers.

Appendix B

Adapted Frayer Model

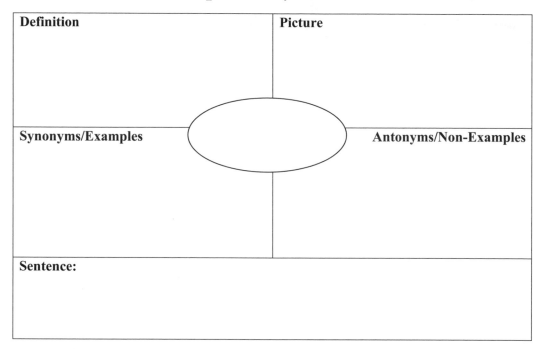

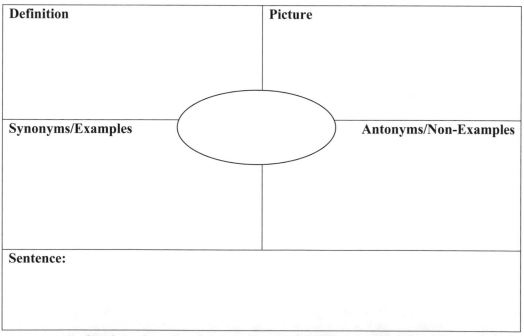

Appendix C

Vocabulary Journal Table of Contents

Name:_____

THEME	DATE	WORD	NOTES	PAGE#

Appendix D

Adapted Frayer Model for English Language Learners

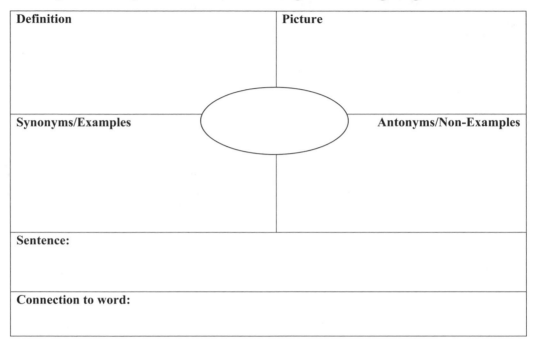

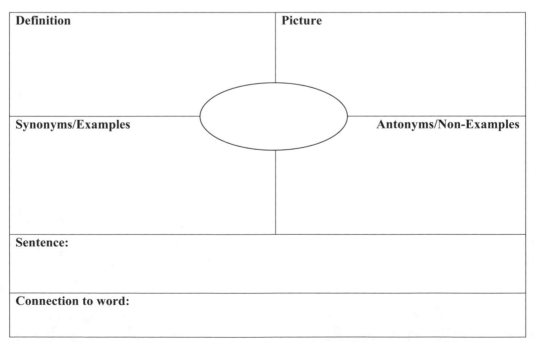

Appendix E

Three-Column Word Chart

Vocabulary Word	Synonyms (Examples)	Antonyms (Non-Examples)

Appendix F

Peer- and Self-Evaluation Form
for PowerPoint Vocabulary Portrayals

Your Name: _____

Peer Evaluator: _____

Date: _____

Social Studies Vocabulary—PowerPoint Portrayal Presentation

Directions: Compare your work with the standards we have set. Be very honest!

1 – I did a thorough job. This reflects excellence!

2 – I did a good job, but I could have done a better job in this area.

NY – Not yet! I need to go back and work on this a bit more to improve.

Qualities of an excellent presentation:	My evaluation of my presentation	Peer evaluation of my presentation	Teacher's evaluation of my project
I made eye contact with the group.			
I did not face the screen while I was talking.			
I did not stand in front of the screen.			
I projected my voice.			
I articulated words so I was easy to understand.			
I explained my slide in detail.			
When I was listening, I practiced SLANT.			
I asked clarifying and probing questions when appropriate.			

Adapted from Riddle (2009)

Additional comments:

Appendix G

Graphic Organizer for Crystal Ball Words

Name: _____   Date: _____

Crystal Ball Words

WORD:		
Prefix:	Root:	Suffix:
Prefix definition:	Root definition:	Suffix definition:
Other words with this prefix:	Other words with this root:	Other words with this suffix:

Word Nerds: Teaching All Students to Learn and Love Vocabulary by Brenda J. Overturf, Leslie H. Montgomery, and Margot Holmes Smith. ©2013. Stenhouse Publishers.

Appendix H

Vocabulary Progress Form

Directions: Record student names in the appropriate boxes for each vocabulary cycle or use one form per student to record anecdotal notes.

Vocabulary Cycle: **Date:**

Demonstrates . . .	Mastered	Almost Mastered	Not Yet Mastered
Appropriate use of vocabulary word in sentences of seven or more words			
Ability to determine meanings of vocabulary words in context			
Ability to determine word relationships (synonyms/examples, antonyms/non-examples)			
Ability to determine nuances in word meaning (shades of meaning)			
Ability to interpret literal or nonliteral or figurative language (similes, metaphors, idioms)			
Understanding of affixes and roots as clues to meaning of a word			
Understanding of use of reference materials			
Higher-order thinking about vocabulary			
Application of vocabulary words outside of vocabulary instruction (in conversation or in other student work)			

References

Children's Literature

Banks, K. 2006. *Max's Words*. New York: Farrar, Straus and Giroux.

Baylor, B. 1995. *I'm in Charge of Celebrations*. New York: Aladdin Picture Books.

Bryant, J. 2008. *A River of Words: The Story of William Carlos Williams*. Grand Rapids, MI: Eerdmans Books for Young Readers.

Clements, A. 1996. *Frindle*. New York: Atheneum.

DeGross, M. 1998. *Donovan's Word Jar*. New York: Amistad.

Finchler, J. 2003. *Testing Miss Malarkey*. Logan, IA: Perfection Learning.

Fine, E. H. 2004. *Cryptomania! Teleporting into Greek and Latin with the Cryptokids*. New York: Tricycle Press.

Frasier, D. 2000. *Miss Alaineus: A Vocabulary Disaster*. San Diego: Harcourt.

Johnson, A. 2005. *A Sweet Smell of Roses*. New York: Simon and Schuster.

Juster, N. 2010. *The Odious Ogre*. New York: Michael diCapua Books.

Kennedy, K. 2007. *Pirate Pete's Talk Like a Pirate*. New York: Abrams Books for Young Readers.

Martin, J. 1989. *Snowflake Bentley*. Boston: Houghton Mifflin.

Rappaport, D. 2001. *Martin's Big Words: The Life of Martin Luther King, Jr.* New York: Hyperion Books.

Riordan, R. 2005. *The Lightning Thief.* Percy Jackson and the Olympians Series Number 1. New York: Hyperion.

Say, A. 1993. *Grandfather's Journey.* Boston: Houghton Mifflin Books for Children.

Schotter, R. 2006. *The Boy Who Loved Words.* New York: Schwartz & Wade.

Scieszka, J. 2001. *Baloney, Henry P.* New York: Viking.

Shannon, D. 1998. *A Bad Case of Stripes.* New York: Blue Sky Press.

Sis, P. 2000. *Starry Messenger: Galileo Galilei.* New York: Square Fish.

Snicket, L. 2010. *13 Words.* New York: HarperCollins.

Steinberg, L. 2005. *Thesaurus Rex.* Cambridge, MA: Barefoot Books.

Teague, M. 2004. *Detective LaRue: Letters from the Investigation.* New York: Scholastic.

Weisner, D. 1992. *June 29, 1999.* Boston: Clarion Books.

Professional Resources

Afflerbach, P. 2012. *Understanding and Using Reading Assessment, K–12.* Newark, DE: International Reading Association.

Alber, S. R., and C. R. Foil. 2003. "Drama Activities That Promote and Extend Your Students' Vocabulary Proficiency." *Intervention in School & Clinic* 39 (1): 22–29.

Allen, J. 1999. *Words, Words, Words: Teaching Vocabulary in Grades 4–12.* York, ME: Stenhouse.

Allen, J., and K. Gonzalez. 1998. *There's Room for Me Here: Literacy Workshop in the Middle School.* York, ME: Stenhouse.

Anderson, R. C. 1990. *Teachers and Independent Reading.* Champaign-Urbana, IL: Center for the Study of Reading.

Anderson, R. C., and W. E. Nagy. 1991. "Word Meanings." In *Handbook of Reading Research*, Vol. II), ed. R. Barr, M. L. Kamil, P. B. Mosenthal, and P. D. Pearson. New York: Longman.

Arter, L. M., and A. P. Nilsen. 2009. "Using Lemony Snicket to Bring Smiles to Your Vocabulary Lessons." *The Reading Teacher* 63 (3): 235–238.

Atwell, N. 1987. *In the Middle: Writing, Reading, and Learning with Adolescents.* Portsmouth, NH: Heinemann.

Baylor, B. 1995. *I'm in Charge of Celebrations.* New York: Aladdin Picture Books.

Bean, R. M., and A. Swan Dagen. 2006. "Vocabulary Assessment: A Key to Planning Vocabulary Instruction." In *Vocabulary-Enriched Classroom: Practices for Improving the Reading Performance of All Students in Grades 3 and Up,* ed. J. Mangieri and C. Collins Block. New York: Scholastic.

Bear, D. R., M. Invernizzi, S. R. Templeton, and F. R. Johnston. 2008. *Words Their Way: Word Study for Vocabulary and Spelling Instruction.* 4th ed. Upper Saddle River, NJ: Prentice Hall.

Beck, I. L., and M. G. McKeown. 2001. "Text Talk: Capturing the Benefits of Read-Aloud Experiences for Young Children." *The Reading Teacher* 55 (1): 10–20.

Beck, I. L., M. G. McKeown, and L. Kucan. 2002. *Bringing Words to Life: Robust Vocabulary Instruction.* New York: Guilford Press.

Beers, K. 2003. *When Kids Can't Read: What Teachers Can Do.* Portsmouth, NH: Heinemann.

Biemiller, A. 2004. "Teaching Vocabulary in the Primary Grades: Vocabulary Instruction Needed." In *Vocabulary Instruction: Research to Practice*, ed. J. F. Baumann and E. J. Kame'enui. New York: Guilford.

Biemiller, A., and C. Boote. 2006. "An Effective Method for Building Vocabulary in Primary Grades." *Journal of Educational Psychology* 98 (1): 44–62.

Bintz, W. P., and S. D. Moore. 2002. "Using Literature to Support Mathematical Thinking in the Middle School." *Middle School Journal* 34 (2): 25–32.

Bintz, W., P. Wright, and J. Sheffer. 2010. "Using Copy Change with Trade Books to Teach Earth Science." *The Reading Teacher* 64 (2): 106–119.

Blachowicz, C., and P. J. Fisher. 2009. *Teaching Vocabulary in All Classrooms.* 4th ed. Boston: Allyn & Bacon.

Blachowicz, C. L. Z., P. J. L.Fisher, D. Ogle, and S. Watts-Taffe. 2006. "Vocabulary: Questions from the Classroom." *Reading Research Quarterly* 41 (4): 534–539.

Blachowicz, C. L. Z., P. J. L. Fisher, and S. Watts-Taffe. 2005. *Integrated Vocabulary Instruction: Meeting the Needs of Diverse Learners in Grades K–5.* Naperville, IL: Learning Points Associates.

Block, C. C., and J. N. Mangieri, eds. 2006. *The Vocabulary-Enriched Classroom: Practices for Improving Reading Performance of All Students in Grades 3 and Up.* New York: Scholastic.

Borgia, L., and C. Owles. 2009/2010. "Using Pop Culture to Aid Literacy Instruction." *Illinois Reading Council Journal* 38 (1): 47–51.

Bromley, K. 2007. "Nine Things Every Teacher Should Know About Words and Vocabulary Instruction." *Journal of Adolescent and Adult Literacy* 50 (7): 528–537.

———. 2012. *The Next Step in Vocabulary Instruction: Practical Strategies and Engaging Activities That Help All Learners Build Vocabulary and Deepen Comprehension.* New York: Scholastic.

Brown, T., and F. Perry. 1991. "A Comparison of Three Learning Strategies for ESL Vocabulary Acquisition." *TESOL Quarterly* 25: 655–670.

Carey, S. 1978. "The Child as Word Learner." In *Linguistic Theory and Psychological Reality*, ed. M. Halle, J. Bresman, and G. Miller. Cambridge, MA: MIT Press.

Carlisle, J. F., C. McBride-Chang, W. Nagy, and T. Nunes. 2010. "Effects of Instruction in Morphological Awareness on Literacy Achievement: An Integrative Review." *Reading Research Quarterly* 45 (4): 464–483.

Carr, E., P. Dewitz, and J. Patberg. 1989. "Using Cloze for Inference Training with Expository Text." *The Reading Teacher* 42 (6): 380–385.

Carr, E., and K. K. Wixson. 1986. "Guidelines for Evaluating Vocabulary Instruction." *Journal of Reading* 29: 588–595.

Cell Press. 2006. "Pure Novelty Spurs the Brain." *Science Daily*. August 26. www.science-daily.com/releases/2006/08/060826180547.htm.

Chatel, R. G. 2001. "Diagnostic and Instructional Uses of the Cloze Procedure." *New England Reading Association Journal* 37 (1): 3–6.

Clay, M. 1998. *By Different Paths to Common Outcomes*. York, ME: Stenhouse.

Conrad, L. L., M. Matthews, C. Zimmerman, and P. A. Allen. 2008. *Put Thinking to the Test*. Portland, ME: Stenhouse.

Council of Chief State School Officers. 2008. *Attributes of Effective Formative Assessment*. www.ccsso.org/Resources/Programs/Formative_Assessment_for_Students_and_Teachers_(FAST).html.

Coyne, M. D., D. B. McCoach, and S. Kapp. 2007. "Vocabulary Intervention for Kindergarten Students: Comparing Extended Instruction to Embedded Instruction and Incidental Exposure." *Learning Disability Quarterly* 30: 74–88.

Dalton, B., and D. L. Grisham. 2011. "eVoc Strategies: 10 Ways to Use Technology to Build Vocabulary." *The Reading Teacher* 64 (5): 306–317.

Davey, B. 1983. "Think-Aloud: Modeling the Cognitive Processes of Reading Comprehension." *Journal of Reading* 27: 44–47.

Delpit, L. D. 1995. *Other People's Children: Cultural Conflict in the Classroom*. New York: The New Press.

Dickinson, D. K., and P. O. Tabors. 2002. "Fostering Language and Literacy in Classrooms and Homes." *Young Children* (March): 10–18.

Echevarria, J., ed. 1998. *Teaching Language to Minority Students in Elementary School*. Research Brief No. 1. Santa Cruz, CA, and Washington, DC: CREDE.

Finchler, J. 2003. *Testing Miss Malarkey*. Logan, IA: Perfection Learning.

Fine, E. H. 2004. *Cryptomania! Teleporting into Greek and Latin with the Cryptokids*. New York: Tricycle Press.

Frasier, D. 2000. *Miss Alaineus: A Vocabulary Disaster*. San Diego: Harcourt.

Frayer, D., W. C. Frederick, and H. J. Klausmeier. 1969. *A Schema for Testing the Level of Cognitive Mastery*. Madison: Wisconsin Center for Education Research.

Frey, N., and D. Fisher. 2009. *Learning Words Inside and Out: Vocabulary Instruction That Boosts Achievement in All Subject Areas*. Portsmouth, NH: Heinemann.

Fry, E. B. 2004. *The Vocabulary Teacher's Book of Lists*. San Francisco: Jossey-Bass.

Garrison, C. 2009. "Formative Assessment: Debunking the Myths." Podcast, June 4. *Today's Middle Level Educator*. Westerville, OH: National Middle School Association. www.amle.org/Publications/TodaysMiddleLevelEducator/tabid/1409/Default.aspx.

Gfeller, K. E. 1986. "Musical Mnemonics for Learning Disabled Children." *Teaching Exceptional Children* (Fall): 28–30.

Goldenberg, C. 1991. *Instructional Conversations and Their Classroom Application*. Educational Practice Report 2. Santa Cruz, CA: National Center for Research on Cultural Diversity and Second Language Learning.

Goodman, Y. M. 1978. "Kid-Watching: An Alternative to Testing." *National Elementary Principal* 57 (4): 41–45.

Graves, M. F. 2006. *The Vocabulary Book: Learning and Instruction*. New York: Teacher's College Press.

———, ed. 2009. *Essential Readings on Vocabulary Instruction*. Newark, DE: International Reading Association.

Greene, A. H., and G. D. Melton. 2007. *Test Talk: Integrating Test Preparation into Reading Workshop*. Portland, ME: Stenhouse.

Hart, B., and T. R. Risley. 1992. "American Parenting of Language-Learning Children: Persisting Differences in Family-Child Interactions Observed in Natural Home Environments." *Developmental Psychology* 28: 1096–1105.

———. 1995. *Meaningful Differences in the Everyday Experiences of Young American Children*. Baltimore: Paul H. Brookes.

Harvey, S., and A. Goudvis. 2007. *Strategies That Work: Teaching Comprehension for Understanding and Engagement*. 2nd ed. Portland, ME: Stenhouse.

Hayes, D. P., and M. G. Ahrens. 1988. "Vocabulary Simplification for Children: A Special Case of 'Motherese'?" *Journal of Child Language* 15 (2): 395–410.

Hill, K. D. 2009. "Code-Switching Pedagogies and African-American Student Voices: Acceptance and Resistance." *Journal of Adolescent and Adult Literacy* 53 (2): 120–131.

International Dyslexia Association. 2009. *Multisensory Structured Language Teaching*. www.interdys.org/ewebeditpro5/upload/Multisensory_Structured_Language_Teaching_Fact_Sheet_11-03-08.pdf.

Jenkins, J., M. Stein, and K. Wysocki. 1984. "Learning Vocabulary Through Reading." *American Educational Research Journal* 21: 767–788.

Jensen, E. 2009. "Chapter 2: How Poverty Affects Behavior and Academic Performance." Association of Supervision and Curriculum Development. www.ascd.org/publications/books/109074/chapters/How-Poverty-Affects-Behavior-and-Academic-Performance.aspx.

Keene, E., and S. Zimmermann. 1997. *Mosaic of Thought: Teaching Comprehension in a Reader's Workshop*. Portsmouth, NH: Heinemann.

Kennedy, K. 2007. *Pirate Pete's Talk Like a Pirate*. New York: Abrams Books for Young Readers.

Kontovourki, S., and C. Campis. 2010/2011. "Meaningful Practice: Test Prep in a Third Grade Public School Classroom." *The Reading Teacher* 64 (4): 236–245.

Ladson-Billings, G. 1995. "Toward a Culturally Relevant Pedagogy." *American Educational Research Journal* 32 (3): 465–491.

Lane, H. B., and S. A. Allen. 2010. "The Vocabulary-Rich Classroom: Modeling Sophisticated Word Use to Promote Word Consciousness and Vocabulary Growth." *The Reading Teacher* 63 (5): 362–370.

Leahy, S., C. Lyon, M. Thompson, and D. Wiliam. 2005. "Classroom Assessment: Minute by Minute, Day by Day." *Educational Leadership* 63 (3): 19–24.

Lesesne, T. S. 2003. *Making the Match: The Right Book for the Right Reader at the Right Time, Grades 4–12*. Portland, ME: Stenhouse.

Lovelace, S., and S. R. Stewart. 2009. "Effects of Robust Vocabulary Instruction and Multicultural Text on the Development of Word Knowledge Among African-American Children." *American Journal of Speech-Language Pathology* 18: 168–179.

Marulis, L. M., and S. Neuman. 2011. How Do Vocabulary Interventions Affect Young At-Risk Children's Word Learning? A Meta-analytic Review. Paper presented at the Society for Research on Educational Effectiveness, spring conference, Washington, DC.

Marzano, R. 2004. *Building Background Knowledge for Academic Achievement: Research on What Works in Schools*. Alexandria, VA: Association for Supervision and Curriculum Development.

———. 2009. "Six Steps to Better Vocabulary Instruction." *Educational Leadership* 67 (1): 83–84.

Marzano, R. J., D. J. Pickering, and J. E. Pollock. 2001. *Classroom Instruction That Works: Research-Based Strategies for Increasing Student Achievement*. Alexandria, VA: Association for Supervision and Curriculum Development.

McGregor, T. 2007. *Comprehension Connections: Bridges to Strategic Reading*. Portsmouth, NH: Heinemann.

McKeown, M. G. 1993. "Creating Effective Definitions for Young Word Learners." *Reading Research Quarterly* 28: 16–31.

McKeown, M. G., I. L. Beck, R. C. Ormanson, and M. T. Pople. 1985. "Some Effects of the Nature and Frequency of Vocabulary Instruction on the Knowledge and Use of Words." *Reading Research Quarterly* 20: 522–535.

McLaughlin, M. 2009. *Content Area Reading: Teaching and Learning in an Age of Multiple Literacies*. Boston: Allyn & Bacon.

McLaughlin, M., and G. L. DeVoogd. 2004. *Critical Literacy: Enhancing Students' Comprehension of Texts*. New York: Scholastic.

Miller, G., and P. Gildea. 1985. "How to Misread a Dictionary." *AILA Bulletin*. Pisa, Italy: International Association for Applied Linguistics.

Moats, L. 1999. *Teaching Reading Is Rocket Science: What Expert Teachers of Reading Should Know and Be Able to Do*. Washington, DC: American Federation of Teachers.

———. 2000. *Speech to Print: Language Essentials for Teachers*. Baltimore: Paul H. Brooks.

Moore, S., and W. P. Bintz. 2002. "From Galileo to Snowflake Bentley: Using Literature to Teach Inquiry in Middle School Science." *Science Scope* 26 (1): 10–14.

Mountain, L. 2007. "Synonym Success—Thanks to the Thesaurus." *Journal of Adolescent & Adult Literacy* 51 (4): 318–324.

Mullen, R., and L. Wedwick. 2008. "Avoiding the Digital Abyss: Getting Started in the Classroom with YouTube, Digital Stories, and Blogs." *Clearing House* 82 (2): 66–69.

Nagy, W. E., R. C. Anderson, and P. A. Herman. 1987. "Learning Word Meanings from Context During Normal Reading." *American Educational Research Journal* 24: 237–270.

Nagy, W. E., and Herman, P. A. 1987. "Breadth and Depth of Vocabulary Knowledge: Implications for Acquisition and Instruction." In *The Nature of Vocabulary Acquisition*, ed. M. G. McKeown and M. E. Curtis. Hillsdale, NJ: Erlbaum.

Nagy, W. E., and J. A. Scott. 1990. "Word Schemas: Expectations About the Form and Meaning of New Words." *Cognition & Instruction* 7 (2): 105–127.

Nagy, W., and D. Townsend. 2012. "Words as Tools: Learning Academic Vocabulary as Language Acquisition." *Reading Research Quarterly* 47 (1): 91–108.

National Governors Association Center for Best Practices and Council of Chief State School Officers (NGA/CCSSO). 2010. Common Core State Standards: English Language Arts and Literacy in History/Social Studies, Science, and Technical Subjects. Washington, DC: Authors. www.corestandards.org/assets/CCSSI_ELA%20Standards.pdf.

National Institute of Child Health and Human Development. 2000. *Teaching Children to Read: An Evidence-Based Assessment of the Scientific Research Literature on Reading and Its Implications for Reading Instruction.* Report of the National Reading Panel. Washington, DC: National Institute of Child Health and Human Development. www.nichd.nih. gov/publications/nrp/smallbook.cfm.

Ocskus, L. 2009. *Interactive Think-Aloud Lessons: 25 Surefire Ways to Engage Students and Improve Comprehension.* New York: Scholastic.

Osborn, S. 2001. "Picture Books for Young Adult Readers." *The ALAN Review* 28 (3): 24.

Powell, W. R. 1986. "Teaching Vocabulary Through Opposition." *The Journal of Reading* 29: 617–621.

Reinhart, J., and R. Martinez. 1996. "Teaching Mainstreamed Dyslexic Students." In *How to Become a Better Reading Teacher*, ed. L. Putnam. Englewood, NJ: Merrill.

Rickford, J., and R. Rickford. 2000. *Spoken Soul: The Story of Black English.* New York: John Wiley & Sons.

Riddle, J. 2009. *Engaging the Eye Generation: Visual Literacy Strategies for the K–5 Classroom.* Portland, ME: Stenhouse.

Rieg, S. A., and K. R. Paquette. 2009. "Using Drama and Movement to Enhance English Language Learners' Literacy Development." *Journal of Instructional Psychology* 36 (2): 148–154.

Riordan, R. 2005. *The Lightning Thief.* Percy Jackson and the Olympians Series Number 1. New York: Hyperion.

Roediger, H. L., and A. C. Butler. 2011. "The Critical Role of Retrieval Practice in Long-Term Retention." *Trends in Cognitive Sciences* 15 (1): 20–27.

Roediger, H. L., and J. D. Karpicke. 2006. "The Power of Testing Memory: Basic Research and Implications for Educational Practice." *Perspectives on Psychological Science* 1: 181–210.

Rowe, M. B. 1986. "Wait Time: Slowing Down May Be a Way of Speeding Up!" *Journal of Teacher Education* 37: 43–50.

Scott, J. A., and W. E. Nagy. 1989. "Fourth Graders' Knowledge of Definitions and How They Work." Paper presented at the annual meeting of the National Reading conference, Austin, TX, December.

Shannon, D. 1998. *A Bad Case of Stripes*. New York: Blue Sky Press.

Siller, J. 1957. "Socioeconomic Status and Conceptual Thinking." *The Journal of Abnormal and Social Psychology* 55 (3): 365–371.

Smith, F. 1987. *Joining the Literacy Club: Further Essays into Education*. Portsmouth, NH: Heinemann.

Sobolak, M. 2011. "Modifying Robust Vocabulary Instruction for the Benefit of Low-Socioeconomic Students." *Reading Improvement* 48 (1): 14–23.

Stahl, K. A. D., and M. A. Bravo. 2010. "Contemporary Classroom Vocabulary Assessment for Content Areas." *The Reading Teacher* 66 (7): 566–578.

Stahl, S. A. 1999. *Vocabulary Development*. Cambridge, MA: Brookline Books.

———. 2003. "Words Are Learned Incrementally Over Multiple Exposures." *American Educator* 27 (1): 18–19.

Stahl, S. A., and M. M. Fairbanks. 1986. "The Effects of Vocabulary Instruction: A Model-Based Meta-analysis." *Review of Educational Research* 56 (1): 72–110.

Stahl, S. A., and W. E. Nagy. 2006. *Teaching Word Meanings*. Mahwah, NJ: Lawrence Erlbaum.

Stanovich, K. 1986. "Matthew Effects in Reading: Some Consequences of Individual Differences in the Acquisition of Literacy." *Reading Research Quarterly* 21: 360–401.

Stone, B. J., and V. Urquhart. 2008. *Remove Limits to Learning with Systematic Vocabulary Instruction*. Denver, CO: Mid-continent for Research in Education and Learning (McREL).

Storm, W. 2006. *Write Up a Storm! Writing Curriculum*. www.writeupastorm.com/.

Templeton, S., D. R. Bear, M. Invernizzi, and F. Johnson. 2010. *Vocabulary Their Way: Word Study with Middle and Secondary Students*. Boston: Pearson.

Tharp, R. G., and R. Gallimore. 1988. "Rousing Schools to Life." *American Educator* 13 (2): 20–25, 46–52.

———. 1991. *The Instructional Conversation: Teaching and Learning in Social Activity.* Research Report 2. Santa Cruz, CA: The National Center for Research on Cultural Diversity and Second Language Learning.

Thomason, D. 2000. *The Animals' Wishes.* Rigby Literacy Big Book, Grade 2. Boston: Houghton Mifflin Harcourt.

Tompkins, G. E. 2003. *Literacy for the 21st Century.* 3rd ed. Upper Saddle River, NJ: Merrill Prentice-Hall.

Wadlington, E. 2000. "Effective Language Arts Instruction for Students with Dyslexia." *Preventing School Failure* 44 (2): 61–65.

Wallace, W. 1994. "Memory for Music: Effect of Melody on Recall of Text." *Journal of Experimental Psychology: Learning, Memory, and Cognition* 20 (6): 1471–1485.

Walters, J. 2006. "Methods of Teaching Inferring Meaning from Context." *Regional Language Centre Journal* 37 (2): 176–190.

Watts, S. M. 1995. "Vocabulary Instruction During Reading Lessons in Six Classrooms." *Journal of Reading Behavior* 27 (3): 399–424.

White, C. E., and J. S. Kim. 2009. *Putting the Pieces of the Puzzle Together: How Systematic Vocabulary Instruction and Extended Learning Time Can Address the Literacy Gap*. Washington, DC: Center for American Progress.

White, T. G., M. F. Graves, and W. H. Slater. 1990. "Development of Recognition and Reading Vocabularies in Diverse Sociolinguistic and Educational Settings." *Journal of Educational Psychology* 82: 281–290.

Wilhelm, J. 1997. *"You Gotta Be the Book": Teaching Engaged and Reflective Reading with Adolescents.* New York: Teachers College Press.

Index

Page numbers followed by an *f* indicate figures.